THE PLACE

DISCOVERING GOD WHERE LIFE HURTS MOST

PATTY MORENO

Cover Design: Moreno Media | Kolton and Dallas Moreno

Cover Painting: Briley Moreno

Literary consulting, editing, and formatting, by Clara Rose & Company.

Published by RoseDale Publishing
14510 Hudson Ave
Spring Hill Florida 34610

ISBN-13: 979-8-9998796-3-9

PRAISE FOR THE PLACE

Patty Moreno's writing is real, raw and redemptive. And she points to the one place we find hope for our souls—The Place! This book will touch your soul from the first page. Let your healing journey begin with page one!

—MARK BATTERSON, New York Times bestselling author of The Circle Maker

The Place does not address your pain with pithy principles… but a pathway to wholeness! Patty's story will point to your story…which will allow God to write a new story!

—DR JEREMY JOHNSON, President, Northwest University

Those who have experienced soul-crushing loss and the avalanche of grief that follows will not find neat theological formulas in these pages. Instead, In The Place, Patty Moreno becomes a scarred-but-healed companion for the painful journey no one wants to take, gently pointing readers to the hope that God Himself is the place where our deepest wounds are seen, tended, and transformed.

— Dr. Jodi Detrick, Speaker, Certified CoachFormer Columnist for The Seattle Times Author of The Jesus-Hearted Woman: 10 Leadership Qualities for Enduring & Endearing Influence, and The Settled Soul: Tenaciously Abiding with a Tender God

Patty writes about the places we never planned to go—hurt, fear, and heartbreak—and the grace of God that meets us there. This book is a beautiful reminder that even the hardest places can become places of healing and hope.

— DR ***WEST DAVIS, Lead Pastor, newlife – Author of people becoming the church***

DEDICATION

To my precious Karissa…

your life mattered.

To The Good Shepherd—

The Lamb of God

who laid down Your Life

for every broken heart

and broken story…

including mine.

THE PLACE

CONTENTS

Lord, you have been our dwelling place
in all generations.
Before the mountains were brought forth,

or ever you had formed the earth and the world,
from everlasting to everlasting you are God.

Psalm 90:1-2(ESV)

INTRODUCTION

Certain days change all our days. January 8,1987 changed mine. A tragedy beyond my power to alter, reshaped me.

In the early days of grief, I whispered to a friend, brave enough to stand beside me, *"I never imagined I would be in this place."*

Maybe you can relate. Perhaps you've endured a devastating loss and now feel crushed beneath a weight of questions that refuse to release you: *Will I ever be free from this senseless tangle of pain*? *How does one survive a broken heart—or breathe beneath the choking cords of despair?*

Are you limping on wounds decades old… defeated by your inability to outpace the pain or recover the missing pieces of your crushed dreams—your shattered heart?

I wrote this book for you.

Your wounded heart, your withered soul, matter profoundly to the One who formed you in the womb and fashioned all your days. (In these moments that fact may feel impossible to embrace.)

The circumstances that brought you to these pages are not hidden from God's view—nor beyond His power to heal.

God is ***The Place*** where healing becomes possible. He offers salve for every heart scraped raw with pain. He embraces the razor-sharp, misshapen fragments of your story. He gives His best—even when you are at your worst.

The One called ***The Place*** invites you to pound His chest with your gnawing questions, to release those crushing burdens, and rest your weary head. He will receive it all. He is listening—continually—for the sound of *your* voice.

Within these pages, I offer personal accounts of His involvement in my story. Some parts may be hard to read or hit too close to home. Others may sound incredibly foreign and hard to reconcile with your own story. My hope is that, despite the various emotions you encounter, you might become increasingly aware of God's presence with you. May every vulnerable account soften the cutting edges of your despair and tune your ears to the frequency of His voice—especially in the moments you feel most abandoned.

Before we begin this journey together, I want to address the nature of this book. It is not a roadmap. It is not a formula for healing, faith, or peace. I simply desire to offer companionship as you walk your hard story and provide hope as I share my story with you. This book holds my story of how God met me—slowly and often unexpectedly—along my own imperfect, winding path of loss.

Your journey will not look like mine. The timing will be different. The questions may be different. The places God draws near may surprise you in ways this book never names. My aim is not to prescribe a way forward, but to bear witness to the creative, tender ways God draws near to broken hearts—and helps us discover we are not alone.

My prayer over you is that The Hands that formed life from dust in Genesis will reach into the dust-heap of your shattered heart to shape something beautiful from your pain.

God cannot heal who we pretend to be. He can only heal our *real* lives. So, if you struggle to trust Him, tell Him.

Your prayer may sound something like this: *"Oh Father, what if I don't know how to trust You? I'm not sure You are a safe place in this dark abyss. But I am so lost—I am so tired—perhaps… I need You. Can You help me even when I don't know how to open my heart to You—even when I resist You—even when belief comes hard? Please, breathe into my soul that I might find strength to take the next step into this moment—with You. Amen.*

Beloved, nothing is so broken it can't be healed.

You are not so lost that Jesus doesn't know where to find you.

When I couldn't outrun the pain, the One called *The Place* ran to me—offering refuge from the storm and freedom to grieve honestly. What I once believed was the end became the beginning of my deepest discovery of the God who redeems our past and rewrites our future.

In Scripture, ***The Place*** is a sacred name for God.

Ancient worshippers used it to describe the nearness of His presence in their most vulnerable moments. In dangerous times, people fled from exposed villages to fortified cities for refuge. That lived experience became language for the safety, provision, and mercy of God.

They declared:

He alone is my refuge, my place of safety;
He is my God, and I trust him.
Psalm 91:1-2 (NLT)

Lord, you have been ***our dwelling place*** *throughout all generations…*
From everlasting to everlasting
You are God.
Psalm 90:1-2 (NIV)

You are ***my hiding place****;*
you protect me from trouble.
You surround me with joyful shouts of deliverance.
Psalm 32:7 (CSB)

These psalmists testified to a God who steps into impossible places and rewrites human stories. And because Jesus is the same, *yesterday, today, and forever (see Hebrews 13:8),* He is just as involved in *your* story.

Right now—while you hold this book in your hands—you are being held. The One who holds the stars in place is holding you.

He knows how to reclaim *your* past and rewrite *your* future.

Breathe deeply.

Beauty Awaits,

Patty

SECTION ONE

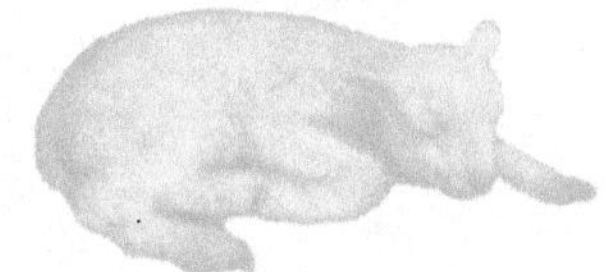

The Shattering

We are brought down to the dust;
our bodies cling to the ground.
Rise up and help us; rescue us
because of your unfailing love.

Psalm 44:25-26 NIV

CHAPTER 1

WHEN TRAGEDY STRIKES

Has the Lord rejected me forever?
Will he never again be kind to me?
Is his unfailing love gone forever?
Have his promises permanently failed?
Has God forgotten to be gracious?
Has he slammed the door on his compassion?
Psalm 77:7-9 (NLT)

Sometimes life burns so hot, one can forget winter's frigid air and the bite of frost under her bare feet. Life can strip the soul so bare; she feels no shame while standing half-dressed in the center of the road.

The high-pitched wail of the siren ripped through the morning hush, jolting an entire neighborhood from its slumber. For the first time in my life, the eerie sound of the distant siren incited comfort over alarm. It signaled hope to my soul. By the time the ambulance rounded the corner onto our street, elderly neighbors, donned in slippers and housecoats, lined the street like spectators anticipating a parade. My arms waved frantically like a flag in the wind—a feeble attempt to expedite its arrival.

It felt like an eternity had passed since my husband's screams yanked me from my slumber. The piercing sound of our daughter's name struck like a dagger through my heart. Never had her name triggered fear. We chose that name as a testament to God's goodness. Karissa. It means grace. The kind of grace that describes

God's favor bursting through the fallow soil of our lives. She was His miracle within my barren womb. Her life painted prisms of delight across our young hearts: bright blue eyes capturing ours, grins welcoming, laughter overflowing, muscles stabilizing, rolling, crawling across space… into the deepest places of our hearts. Seven months flew by—each day an amplification of God's love.

Against my husband's better judgment, Karissa and I arrived home the night before this dreadful morning. We had just returned from an extended Midwest Christmas vacation with my family. Gary had come home a week earlier to work on our home renovations. The day before our flight, he called and suggested we delay our arrival—the gas company couldn't turn on our heat until the end of the week. Without it, our home felt like a grocery store cooler. I assured him that the joy of our reunion would thaw the frigid air within our walls. All we needed were a few extra blankets for a cozy night's rest.

Long after we had tucked Karissa into her crib with extra blankets, we reminisced over photos from her first Christmas; her first tree-cutting, gift-opening, and family feasting. We had even squeezed in a trip to Mount Rushmore. Every familiar tradition felt newly significant through the lens of parenthood.

When she fell asleep, we crawled into bed. I pressed close against my husband, overflowing with contentment and gratitude for this precious family I called mine. Little did I know its landscape would shatter within hours.

When Tragedy Strikes

We slept comfortably, except for Karissa's demand to be nursed at some point during the night. The trip to Grandma and Grandpa's small home had wreaked havoc on her routine. Karissa enjoyed the benefit of the three of us sleeping in the room next to theirs. Determined to keep her from waking my parents, I drew her to my breast whenever she grew restless with her new sleeping arrangements. I was determined to waste no time getting her back on her regular feeding schedule. So, on this first night home, her cries didn't weaken my resolve. As she simmered down, I drifted into a few more hours of deep rest.

It was 6:30 a.m. when Gary kissed my cheek. *"I'm bringing Karissa to bed with us before I head into work,"* he whispered. Those morning snuggles were the sweetest moments of our day. Still intoxicated within the warm comfort of our bed, I mustered up a challenge, *"If you wake her up, Gary, you're nursing her!"*

However, it was not her little body molding into mine that roused me. Moments later, it was Gary's gut-wrenching scream that shattered my slumber. My blood froze in terror. Convinced an intruder had invaded our home, I dove out of our bed, probing my fuzzy brain for a defense strategy—until a second scream ignited my worst fear.

"KA-RIS-SA!"

I bolted down the hall to the nursery. Hunched over her crib, desperate to awaken our little girl, Gary continued screaming her name. Looking into her eyes, I knew something was desperately wrong.

"Patty, she's not breathing." Gary's voice quaked with panic.

The room spun. *"Gary, she is going to be okay."*

Oh, God. Please – help us.

Adrenaline jolted me into action. After calling 9-1-1, I immediately reached out to my brother, Jim, an EMT in South Dakota. While we waited for the paramedics, he guided us through a series of steps to increase her chances of survival. He gave clear instructions over the phone. Stranded at the stationary landline, just out of reach of the nursery, I yelled out each command to my husband. Gary would shout a response, which I would then relay back to Jim.

"Tell Gary to find her pulse."

"HE CAN'T FIND ONE, JIM."

"Feel for air from her mouth or nostrils."

"GARY DOESN'T FEEL ANY AIR."

Open her mouth and begin breathing air into her lungs until the paramedics arrive.

"OH GOD, PLEASE SEND US HELP."

I refused to fully grasp the horror of the moment. I slammed the phone down and ran into the street, just as the distant wail of the ambulance pierced the air. A growing crowd of onlookers stood frozen, staring in disbelief as they watched me wave frantically. Most of them were decades older than us. Confusion twisted their faces. What could possibly drive a young couple in their twenties to call for an ambulance?

The paramedics quickly ushered Gary out of the nursery and worked feverishly on Karissa, launching the defibrillator as we cried out to God from our bedroom.

Moments later, they told me to throw on clothes and shoes, I would ride with Karissa in the ambulance. With room for only one passenger, a paramedic placed his hand on Gary's shoulder, "I need you to drive carefully. We don't need two tragedies today."

A wave of hope washed over me as I climbed aboard. The ambulance was fully equipped for an emergency like ours. Karissa would receive everything she needed on the way to the hospital. "*Thank you, Father.*" I pushed fear aside, anchoring my thoughts on God's goodness and infinite power. His presence flooded that noisy, rolling chapel. I felt His peace. I wondered if the paramedics sensed it. Without interruption, they listened as I lifted my voice to God, thanking Him for His presence and pleading for His mercy.

Upon arrival, I watched helplessly as they wheeled Karissa into the hospital on a gurney ten times too big for her. The bite of the freezing air deepened my agony. Why weren't they shielding her from the cold, holding her close, or wrapping her in a blanket? Instead, they rushed through the automatic doors, escorting her toward warmth and safety.

The following moments felt like a scene from that old science-fiction TV series, *The Twilight Zone.*[i] I could hear the receptionist's questions, but couldn't string words together to form coherent answers. *"May we have your full name, address, phone number, and insurance carrier?"*

Are you kidding me? My odds of retrieving this information rivaled the odds of remembering my high school locker combination. Finally, Gary arrived and, with calm determination, filled in the missing details.

A member of the medical team escorted us into a small room and informed us a doctor would be in shortly with an update. Another deep breath. I felt profoundly grateful for this special treatment. The quiet room offered a sense of privacy and security. My limited life experience offered no context for this space. How could I have known it was reserved for those who needed space to grieve?

As news of our situation reached the households of dear friends, the doctor delivered updates to an ever-growing audience. His first report was measured: "*Mr. and Mrs. Moreno, I want to assure you, we are doing all we can.*" On his second visit, his tone had shifted: *"Mr. and Mrs. Moreno, we are continuing to work with your daughter, but it is not looking good."*

Each time the doctor left the room, I clung to any thread of hope woven into his words, searching for reassurance. Another long lapse of time. Surely, they wouldn't still be working on her if she were gone. That meant Karissa was still fighting.

My thoughts were racing, *Oh God, Karissa needs your strength right now. You declare, "Death is swallowed up in victory. Oh, death, where is your victory? Death, where is your sting?"* (1 Corinthians 15:54b-55). *Jesus, you conquered death so Karissa might experience victory over it. Please, let her experience your victory over death right now. I ask this in Your name.*

Anchors of faith dug deep into the bedrock of all I knew to be true about God. I loved Him. I had experienced His power and provision countless times over the past twenty-three years. Even now, I knew—beyond a doubt—He heard me.

No prayer, no faith, no wall of support could brace me for the moment the doctor walked in for the final time. The room held its breath. Every eye fixed on him, waiting, dreading. It felt like my heart was beating outside my chest. Life and death hung in the balance of this announcement.

He remained silent.

Please, say something, my mind screamed.

Slowly, he lifted his head, his eyes locking onto ours. *"Mr. and Mrs. Moreno, we have done all we know to do."* Each word fell like a single note in a dissonant chord, slow and fractured, pausing after each one. *"Even if we had been successful..."* Another long pause, sucking the air from the room, "*Your daughter's brain was deprived of the oxygen needed to thrive."*

Then his words shattered my world, *"Your daughter... is deceased. I am so deeply sorry. There is nothing more I can do."*

Despite all I knew of God's goodness, my grip failed. The shield of faith grew too heavy, slipping from my hands and crashing to the ground. And then – impact. The explosion shattered my heart into jagged pieces, scattering in every direction.

Agonized screams ricocheted off the walls. Guttural, unearthly wails; sounds reserved for the most unbearable moments of life filled the room. Then, a chilling realization struck me. The screams were mine.

Every muscle in my body collapsed under the weight of his words. Our friends pressed in around us, as if their embrace could compress the deadly hemorrhage of our shattered hearts. The two paramedics who had carried her from our home now stepped into the room. They did not speak. They did not need to. Their silent presence folded into our grief, their tears mingling with ours.

I could not fathom leaving the confines of this tightly packed space. Crossing its threshold meant stepping into a world without Karissa; an existence I could not bear to face.

But our circle of trusted friends knew when it was time. Gently, they guided us, through heavy doors, into a world drained of color, stripped of oxygen. Each step forward widened the impossible gap between our girl and us. And for the first, unthinkable time in seven months, we left her behind—alone—in the hands of strangers.

My fragile mind insisted this was only a nightmare, one I could wake from if I just tried hard enough. Desperate to anchor myself in reality, I replayed the previous twenty-four hours.

Less than twelve hours ago, Karissa had charmed flight attendants and fellow passengers with her belly laughs and ear-to-ear grins. At the diner, on our way home, Gary moved salt and pepper shakers out of her relentless reach. Just hours ago, her squeals filled our home as she tried to out-crawl her chasing daddy. Her tiny fingers curled around mine as I nursed her and laid my perfectly healthy girl in her crib.

But these memories twisted into self-accusation and pleas tangled with regret.

Why didn't I run to her the moment she cried to be fed? I could have stopped this. O God, I beg You – let me hear her cry. Let me run to her. Please, wake me from this nightmare. One sound. Just one simple sound could release my soul from its agony.

But no cry came. No awakening. Only silence, dragging us deeper into the inky blackness of an unwanted reality.

Gary and I slumped in the backseat of our friend's car. *"Are you driving us home?"* My voice trembled.

I was terrified of that chamber of death. Yet desperation for Karissa's belongings demanded I cross its threshold. I longed for her photo album, her clothes still sweet with her scent, my journal; anything that might bring me closer to her, if only for a moment. So, we entered the emptiness—a place once bursting with joy. I clutched each item to my face, trying to inhale life itself. Instead, anguish overflowed the banks of my soul.

Within hours, my family arrived from all over the country. Friends scrambled to arrange their housing, knowing they, too, needed triage for their bleeding hearts. I could only hope someone else would stop the hemorrhaging. In shock and disbelief, they grieved with us, sharing memories of Karissa's charm and laughter. That brief Christmas holiday held the only memories they would ever hold. I feared how swiftly each picture would fade.

How could life unravel so completely in a single day? Did this nightmare have no limits?

Our pastors opened their home to two souls, scared spitless. It became a fortress, its gates yielding to endless waves of grief. With each passing hour, those waves intensified.

The throbbing pain of engorged breasts marked time. I counted Karissa's missed feedings, each one a fresh wound. I poured every ounce of energy into recalling her scent, her lively blue eyes, her velvet skin, and the weight of her body bundled in my arms. But grief was relentless. Emotional aftershocks seized every muscle, leaving me paralyzed beneath their grip.

Gong. Gong. Gong. Twelve ominous chimes, a monotone score to a life without melody. The grandfather clock in our friend's home became a cruel herald, announcing every torturous hour.

Time marched on—unstoppable—carving a path into a dark unknown. Just as I drifted into a fitful state of rest, the towering clock pronounced another hour of separation. Tears re-emerged, spilling into my ears, and saturating my pillow. One script connected all of them: *Karissa. Baby girl. Forgive me. I wasn't there to help you. I can't live without you.*

This agony eclipsed even the physical pain of engorgement. The suffocating crush of grief battled lungs desperate to expand. The room lacked oxygen. I resolved to watch for the faintest shadows of dawn. Perhaps the wings of a new day would carry hope.

Morning arrived. But the sunlight did not bring relief—it burned like an interrogation lamp, exposing the depth of our tragedy.

This nightmare was real. *This* was my life.

CHAPTER 2

NOT MY WILL

The LORD is close to the brokenhearted
and saves those who are crushed in spirit.
Psalm 34:18 (NIV)

That first morning after Karissa's death exposed more than our tragedy—it exposed my desperation. I had no map for this kind of sorrow. No strategy. No strength of my own. I wasn't searching for explanations. I needed air. I needed a way to survive the next minute, the next hour—this impossible day without her.

My grief was too raw for tidy explanations or spiritual platitudes. Questions piled higher than the clouds—but what I ached for was God Himself.

Someone had dropped off a small booklet, *The Death of a Little Child* by J. Vernon McGee. I'll never forget that moment. Gary leaned over the tub and softly read every comforting page aloud while I soaked in the hot water, trying to stop the tremors and letting the tears come without restraint.

In those early hours, I couldn't imagine how many others had walked this same road. I would slowly discover that my story wasn't isolated. One day I would understand how pain touches every life in different ways. Loss, heartbreak, and despair are inescapable realities. If you're carrying a heavy story—if catastrophic loss has upended *your* life—you know this. Like me, you may not be in a mental space for spiritual answers... You may simply be trying to breathe.

I was there.

All I had left was a trembling love and a broken heart. Yet even there, one undeniable truth tethered me to solid ground: the same Savior who wept at gravesides and carried His own cross would now carry me.

This is true for you as well. In your suffering, Jesus—the suffering Savior—holds you. He endured His own agony so He could walk with you through yours.

He understands suffering. Before He was even crucified, the depth of His anguish was overwhelming. One disciple had betrayed Him. Within hours, another would deny Him, and the rest would run for their lives. He was left to suffer all alone—abandoned by His closest friends.

Earlier that evening, Jesus had led those friends to one of His most cherished places of prayer—the Garden of Gethsemane (Mark 14:66-72). While they slept, He carried the crushing weight of fear, isolation, and betrayal. His grief was so intense that His sweat mingled with blood. The medical field has a name for that now: it's a rare condition known as hematohidrosis.[ii] Even before shedding His blood on the cross, His compassion flowed to heal your wounds. His flesh groaned against the injustice of sin and suffering.

In that garden, He uttered a desperate prayer; recorded, perhaps, for our benefit.

...He fell to the ground and prayed that, if possible, the hour might pass from him. "Abba, Father," He said, "everything is possible for you. Take this cup from me. Yet not what I will, but what you will."
Mark 16:35-36 (NIV)

Like many of us, Jesus begged God to change His circumstance. Yet, knowing His Father's heart, He surrendered to His will. In becoming fully human, He not only tasted our suffering, but He was qualified to redeem it. He allowed Himself to be broken so we could be healed.

During a recent visit to the Holy Land, I stood in what is believed to be this garden of suffering—Gethsemane. Of all the places on the tour, this was one of my favorites. Just outside the crowded city of Jerusalem, it was a quiet, unassuming space; beautiful, yet not breathtaking. And yet, as I stood there, I could hardly breathe. I felt the great battle Jesus was willing to wage for my healing. In this very place, the course of human history… of my history… shifted.

Sin and suffering began in the garden of Eden,[iii] but here… in Gethsemane, the unraveling of sin's curse began. In Eden, humanity defied the Father's will (Genesis 3). In Gethsemane, the Son of Man knelt and declared, *"Not my will, but Yours be done"* (Luke 22:44). In the first garden, Adam's rebellion led to death. In this garden, Christ's surrender opened the gate to eternal life (John 10).[iv]

Fully clothed in humanity, Jesus picked up our bitter cup of suffering. He saw *your* face, *your* devastation, *your* sin, *your* doubts, *your* anger, *your* anguish—and embraced the Father's desire to restore *you* to Himself. In this garden, He took upon Himself the full weight of sin's consequence, carrying it to the cross to destroy its power over us.

In my own Gethsemane-garden of suffering, I clung to God's nature and promises, gripping tightly to His Word:

> *"You can ask for anything in my name, and I will do it,*
> *so that the Son can bring glory to the Father."*
> *John 14:13* (NLT)

This verse gave me permission to ask—so I did, again and again. I pleaded for a miracle, for deliverance from the pain, for God's glory to be revealed in my devastation.

To me, the answer seemed clear—Karissa's resurrection.

Since Jesus Himself asked for the impossible more than once, I followed His example. I desired God's will above my own, never expecting it would look so different from what I hoped. I begged for Karissa's life to be restored, for life to return to me. Each morning, I woke up believing, today would be the day… my miracle would come.

Scripture promises:

If you say, "The Lord is my refuge,"
And you make the Most High your dwelling place,
no harm will overtake you,
no disaster will come near your tent.
The Lord says, "I will rescue those who love me.
I will protect those who trust in my name."
Psalm 91:9-10, 14 (NIV)

Most would agree, the death of a loved one is the very definition of harm and disaster. From childhood, He was *The Place* my soul found refuge in. I loved and trusted Him with my whole life. He was the One who had etched these promises on my heart—the One who vowed to protect and rescue.

Based on that promise, I couldn't accept death as the final word over Karissa. So, when my family went to the funeral home, I stayed behind. The images of death would only mock the faith I clung to. Instead, I fixed my eyes on God's promises. I would wait – until Karissa beamed with life once more.

Scripture amplifies God's power over death. I was drawn to the story of Jairus, a father desperate to save his dying daughter. He fell at Jesus' feet, begging for her healing. Jesus agreed to go with him, but before they arrived, the girl died.

Jesus' response? *"Don't be afraid. Just have faith."* (Mark 5:36)

At Jairus' home, the scene was chaotic—mourners wailing, grief filling the air. But Jesus entered and asked,

"Why all this commotion and weeping?
The child isn't dead; she's only asleep."
The crowd laughed at Him. But He made them leave.
Then, taking the girl's parents and His three disciples,
He stepped into the room where she lay.
Holding her hand, He said, "Talitha koum,"
which means, "Little girl, get up!"
And immediately, the twelve-year-old stood and walked around.
The crowd was overwhelmed—completely astonished.
Mark 5:38-42a (NLT)

Jesus' words became the refrain of my soul: "*Don't be afraid. Just have faith.*" I didn't care if the world thought me crazy. I became convinced God's resurrection power was as capable of awakening Karissa as it was to awaken Jairus's girl. A new generation would witness His glory.

My relentless faith had roots. Karissa's life began with a miracle. Tumors on my pituitary gland had stunted the development of my uterus and ovaries, preventing puberty and a menstrual cycle—until the very month she was conceived. Her existence was proof of God's power; surely, her resurrection would magnify it.

From the moment she entered our world, I longed for her life to bring God glory. More than once in prayer, I had sensed Jesus whisper, *"Karissa's life will reach thousands with My unfailing love."* Had I truly heard His voice? If God had spoken, there was no other option. He had to resurrect her.

So—I waited—for one phone call. Minutes turned to hours. Hours to days. Days of endless waiting. Restless nights of shallow sleep, followed by more unrelenting prayers: "Father, please send resurrection news. I know this is impossible for man, but with God, all things are possible." (Matthew 19:26)

As the days passed, the prayer within my soul began to shift: *"Lord, if You are willing, please restore her life. Yet... not my will, but Yours be done."*

CHAPTER 3

BURIED TREASURE

Because of the LORD's great love, we are not consumed,
for his compassions never fail.
They are new every morning;
great is your faithfulness.
I say to myself, "The LORD is my portion;
therefore I will wait for him."
Lamentations 3:22-24 (NIV)

Suffering is a lonely road. Even when grieving the same loss, no two hearts break the same way. My husband's sorrow, as lonely and tumultuous as mine, took a different shape. While I sat for hours by the phone, waiting for a miracle I doggedly hoped for, Gary's agony poured out onto a recording of her lullaby—a song of worship and surrender written seven months earlier for her dedication. His rich voice, now broken and raw with despair, carried a father's steadfast love for his daughter within each note. He had never imagined his lyrics to be prophetic, describing the hardest act of surrender he would ever face. Now, he felt the assurance of God's hand over the lyrics.

One summer's eve I sat to write this song
About a precious little girl who came along.
She blessed my home with so much joy
That I can only say, "My precious Jesus,
I want to dedicate this little life today.

(chorus) Because every day we see her, we see a gift from God;

And every time she cries out loud, Oh Lord, we want to applaud
Your holiness for giving us, our Karissa.
Lord, receive her.

Now as we give her back to You,
Lord, we pray that her greatest dreams come true.
May she know Your voice and see Your light in mommy's life and mine;
And when she runs to You, please let her know that everything will be fine. Inside Your arms.
Lord, keep our daughter from all harm.

(chorus) Because every day we see her, we see a gift from God.
And every time she cries out loud, Oh Lord, I want to applaud
Your holiness, for giving us, our Karissa.
Lord, receive her.[v]

This song formed bookends to two ceremonies—a baby dedication and a funeral—only seven months apart. Her funeral arrived. Seated in the front row, I set my gaze on the One who makes our impossible, possible. Though our hearts felt hollow, a packed auditorium of friends and family filled the vacancy of our grief.

Following the funeral, a small group of family and friends gathered for her burial on a serene hilltop at Forest Lawn in Glendale, California. Ironically, Karissa and I had walked these grounds before; feeding swans, wandering through the famous mausoleum, never imagining the immense sorrow of this place. I failed to recognize the piercing pain of death and burial that shaped these grounds… until now.

We were guided to the hillside where Karissa was to be buried. Then, I saw it—her simple white casket. Our ministry team had arranged every detail of her burial, carrying a weight we were too shattered to bear.

Trembling, I drew near. It was the closest I had been to my girl in nearly a week. It felt like a lifetime since I held her in my arms, the joy of my entire world. Endless tears cascaded onto her small, white casket. Death, it was more than a sting.[vi] It was a crushing weight, threatening to smother my soul. I choked out a whisper, *"Jesus—please.*" I ached for His voice to shatter the silence. *"Little girl, get up!"* Was this the sacred moment He waited for… this opportunity for me to ask, one more time, before witnesses?

I held my tattered journal that cradled a tender, unedited poem of elated praise, written the day test results announced the miracle: *my barren womb thrumming with life.* Wiping away tears that blurred my vision, I read the poem aloud. I was desperate for another God-sized miracle.

A Song From the Heart

Only my Savior could bring life to my womb.
Only a Mighty God could birth life in this tomb.
My body is yours to bring life as You will.
My child is Yours.
In her life, Lord, please dwell.
May this child leap at the sound of Your name.
May she realize the might You displayed when she came.
May she always rely on the strength that You give;
And may she choose throughout life for You only to live.
Oh, Lord Jesus, my Master, I love You so much!
May I never take for granted Your healing touch.[vii]

Through tears, I pleaded with the Author of Life to breathe over this moment. I reminded my soul, and those gathered with us, of Karissa's need of the very same breath that sustained us now. The same power that had awakened life in a barren womb could awaken life here, in this tomb. Jesus—the Life-Giver—was our only hope.

We circled her tiny casket and prayed the most honest, vulnerable prayer of our lives. I don't remember the words; only the raw sincerity of desperate souls. (In hindsight, perhaps my family and friends were praying more for me than for Karissa.)

Time passed. I listened intently. Beyond the murmur of prayers around that circle, I waited for another sound. It never came…

As prayers faded, I became aware, for the first time, of the nearby tractor carrying a stifling load of soil. My dad placed his arm around my shoulder, his words shattering the sacred silence, *"Patty, God is still in control. We need to trust Him.*"

Gary joined him, steadying my limp frame as we descended the hill. With each step, my hope for a miracle dimmed.

Please. I don't want to rush God. May we stay just a few more minutes?

I feared our Treasure would not be the only thing buried on that hill. With each step, I felt a yanking at the roots deep within me: confidence in God's love, childlike hope in His promises, unwavering trust in His power. What if this descent uprooted everything that steadied me? Would my faith become as lifeless as God's *Emblem of Grace*? Would my hope in His goodness suffocate within that black grave?

Time has a way of propelling us forward before we've reconciled the last moment. I longed to silence the chaos in my mind, to hear God's voice speak. His was the hand I yearned to hold, the only One strong enough to steady me on this slippery slope.

From the back window of a vehicle, I gazed one last time at the tiny casket entombing my priceless gift from God. The caretaker, freighted with His load, had no understanding of *The Miracle, The Matchless Treasure,* left alone on that hillside. He had no comprehension of *The Irreplaceable Child* he was scheduled to bury.

God, I know! O Father, I will never understand why You didn't stop this, why You allowed Karissa's life with us to end. I don't understand You, but... You know I love you. Please, don't leave me now. If I don't have You, I have nothing.

An Invitation

In the days and months that followed, I discovered my need to find a way to bring all that lived inside me to God, *My Place of Refuge.* I needed a space to hold all the questions, the fears, and the fragile hopes that I didn't know how (or dared) to speak aloud. Journaling became a way I could wrestle honestly with God and to listen for His voice in the middle of my pain. He was My Place—ready to hold all my pain, longings, anxiety, emptiness, fear, anger and doubts.

What follows is an invitation for you to do the same—I've created journaling prompts in this book for you to meet Him—*The Place of Refuge*—in whatever chapter of life you are walking through.

So, as you come to the end of each section, I want to encourage you to grab your favorite journal and find a quiet space to share the contents of your heart.

INVITING GOD TO BECOME YOUR PLACE

Life has a way of bringing us to our knees, of interrupting the life we know and love. One moment overflows with promise and the next obliterates hope. Perhaps you can relate. Are you trapped in a painful nightmare where questions-without-answers gouge your soul? Maybe you wonder if you will ever find a way out of this black hole?

"Inviting God to Become Your Place" is a space designed to help you encounter God in the moment you're navigating. It offers space to process your journey—the wrestle of your thoughts and feelings; to record mile markers along the way—discoveries of God's heart on your hard pathway.

One day, as you look in the rearview mirror, you may recognize how His presence surrounded you—moment by moment. But that is the future. Jesus knows how hard it is to see Him now—in *this* moment. Simply offer Him your real self—your shattered heart. Resist the temptation to record words you wish you felt. God cannot heal who we pretend to be. He welcomes you to come as you are—and will hold sacred the stuff that has gathered in the depths of your heart.

God yearns to reveal Himself as *Your Place.* He invites us, *"Abide in Me and I will abide in you."* (See John 15:4) In other words, *'Make your home in Me. Stay with Me, and I will stay with you'.* What an offer from the Creator who knows everything about you and loves you completely. He will not belittle your sacred pain or condemn your gnawing questions. I didn't know it then, but over time I discovered our fractures are not final. He does not leave us alone in the storm surrounding us. He offers hope. You are safe here—in His Everlasting Arms.

I invite you, when you feel ready, to read the following passage slowly—perhaps several times—I pray the love God has for you will begin to take root in your heart. May these words help you talk to Him today.

The eternal God is my dwelling-place,
And underneath me are the everlasting arms.
Deuteronomy 33:27 (ESV – personalized)

It may not feel true right now, but God is a safe *Place* to bring your suffering. He will not ignore *your* voice. Perhaps, Jesus called the Holy Spirit our Comforter because He knew we would face life circumstances, leaving us desperate for genuine comfort. The Holy Spirit is able to soothe your searing pain. He is listening—and grieving with you.

Acknowledge your Pain

If you are able, name what hurts. Tell Him what is too heavy or frightening to bear.

Notice What You Feel

What emotions surface as I sit with God in this moment?

Remember His Nearness

You may not *feel* Him, but He is not absent. The Comforter sits beside you, sharing your tears, strengthening your trembling frame.

In the pain, has there been a moment that I sensed—even faintly—that God is with me?

Receive His Invitation

Jesus whispers, “Abide in Me… make your home in Me, and I will remain with you.” This is not a demand—it is an invitation into safety.

What do I hear the Father inviting me to release into His arms today?

Root Yourself in Scripture

When you are ready, read this passage again slowly, perhaps aloud, until it begins to soften the edges of your pain:

“The eternal God is your dwelling place,
and underneath are the everlasting arms.”
— Deuteronomy 33:27 (ESV)

Is there a word or phrase from this passage that speaks to my need today?

Respond Honestly

Talk to God as you are—not the version you hope to be. Not the version others expect. Let this be your unfiltered offering.

My prayer in this place of pain.

Rest in His Arms

God holds sacred the pieces of your shattered heart. He shelters you in His everlasting arms—steady, patient, untiring arms.

Is there any way in which I sense God strengthening, steadying, or holding me today?

SECTION TWO

The Place of Presence

In All My Darkness

The Lord is close to the brokenhearted.
He rescues those whose spirits are crushed!

Psalm 34:18 NIV

CHAPTER 4

INTO THE DARKNESS

The light shines in the darkness,
and the darkness can never extinguish it.
John 1:5 (NLT)

Show Me Where It Hurts

Do you remember when your parent's comforting arms and steady voice were enough to soften the sting of pain?

"Show me where it hurts."

A parent has likely spoken those words more times than she can count—lifting a child onto her lap, inspecting a scraped knee or elbow smacked against concrete.

"Do you need the Boo-boo Bunny?"

The child nods, wiping away tears.

If you've never used a boo-bunny… you're welcome. Seriously. This simple life-hack is a household game-changer. A folded washcloth becomes a healing balm for childhood wounds. (If you're curious, your favorite browser will happily provide folding instructions.)

The bunny arrives holding an ice cube behind its ears—usually doubling as a flavorless popsicle—and hops toward the child with a silly song:

> *I am a booboo bunny, and I hear you have a hurt.*
> *I'm not sure if you fell down on the sidewalk or the dirt.*
> viii

But if you put an ice-cube in the pocket behind my ears,
And put me on the place you hurt. The pain soon disappears.

What a brilliant invention. For less than a dollar, ninety percent of childhood ailments are healed.

If only pain—and its treatment—remained so simple.

Unfortunately, wounds in a grown-up world defy an easy fix. They sink deeper—sometimes so deep they feel catastrophic. The landscape of our lives can change in a single, unsuspecting moment.

Mount Saint Helens was once a majestic mountain in the Pacific Northwest—a breathtaking refuge for hikers and wildlife. Then, on one unsuspecting spring day in 1980, the mountain exploded with a force five-hundred times greater than an atomic bomb. Over a thousand feet of the mountain shattered into dust, decimating life all around it. Surrounding towns looked like war zones.

Reporters used words like *destruction, chaos,* and *the end* to describe the scene. These same words may describe the blow that shattered your heart.

They called it *"a day where life was interrupted, without warning."* This statement struck me as odd. After all, interruptions rarely come with advance notice. Perhaps some moments are so violent, they deserve such redundancy.

Maybe your life was interrupted in a single moment—without warning—without time for your soul to brace itself for the ash-heap you were buried beneath.

As you search the gray landscape for anything familiar, your heart aches for what once was. You know your life will never look the same after the loss, the illness, the betrayal, the diagnosis, the devastating decision.

Choking beneath the suffocating ash of a once-splendid life, you may wonder if beauty will ever return.

In the same way a loving parent runs to a wounded child, God reaches for us in our agony. He doesn't accuse or hurry us. He beckons gently:

"Show me where it hurts."

Our bloodshot eyes meet His eyes of holy fire. We whisper with trembling honesty, *"Everywhere."*

Into The Darkness

I wondered if the darkness might consume me. A loud vortex of questions without answers invaded my hours. I begged God for a way *around* this suffering, but He offered no detour. This valley was mine to walk *through*.

My prayers changed.

They shifted from, *"Jesus, please breathe life into my girl,"* to, *"Jesus, breathe life into me. I need to know You're here on this painful path."*

More than relief, I needed His presence. At the time, I didn't always feel His nearness. One day I would look back—and recognize how near His presence had been in that terrifying darkness. But right now, its intensity was often too acute to recognize His nearness.

The Dark Night of The Soul

To you the night shines as bright as day.
Darkness and light are the same to you.
Psalm 139:12b

When suffering strikes, long days stretch into even longer nights, plunging us into a deep, endless sorrow.

St. John of the Cross, the 16th-century Spanish mystic and poet, called this *the dark night of the soul*—a phrase later used to describe seasons that shake us to the core.

Psychologist Chiara Viscomi calls it a time "*marked by despair, loss of meaning, and deep uncertainty about life and its purpose.*[ix]"

Scripture is honest about these moments; it preserves in its pages the ancient cries of people who wrestled with the very same questions we ask—people who wondered if God had turned away:

Has the Lord rejected me forever?
Will he never again be kind to me?
Is his unfailing love gone forever?
Have his promises permanently failed?
Has God forgotten to be gracious?
Has he slammed the door on his compassion?
And I said, "This is my fate;
the Most High has turned his hand against me.
Psalm 77:7-10 (NLT)

When I first read those words, I didn't analyze them. I heard myself crying out within them.

American author F. Scott Fitzgerald captured the essence of this despair. *"In a real dark night of the soul it is always three o'clock in the morning, day after day."*[x] Who hasn't felt that longing, that waiting—for the darkness to lift?

When I couldn't feel God's nearness, I clung to the words of the psalmist. My own words were gone. Even in the deepest night, I found Scripture didn't leave me without a *Place* to run—it nudged me to keep looking when I felt so alone. When the shadows were longest and the ache felt endless, the psalmist lifted his voice—not to deny the valley, but to reveal Who walked with him in it.

Yea, though I ***walk through*** the valley of the shadow of death,

I will fear no evil; For You are with me...
Psalm 23:4a (NKJV)

It was as though David—a young shepherd turned king—knew it would not always be three o'clock in the morning... *day after day.*

All I could do was hope that one day... I wouldn't be hiding in the dark—from the darkness. It took me a long time to notice something small... but now something felt important:

David didn't say he lived in the valley. He said, though I '*walk through'* it.

That detail mattered to me—because I needed to believe the darkness was not my destination. It was a passage—we all encounter, and one we would never have to walk alone.

Jesus warned us about this life: *"In this world you will have trouble." John 16:33 (NIV)* Dark nights and black valleys are not signs of abandonment. They are inevitable realities of a fallen world. But David offers hope—not by denying suffering or the absence of danger—but by elevating the nature of the Shepherd.

I began to notice David's understanding of the intimacy between a shepherd and his sheep. Even when life's blackest circumstances eclipsed God's presence, he trusted in his Shepherd's unfailing care. While passing through his own valley of death—that darkest, most terrifying stretch of the human story—David remained confident that God would protect, guide, and provide.

I longed for the day I would feel that confidence again.

In the book, *A Shepherd's Look at Psalm 23*[xi], Phillip Keller describes the arduous preparation a shepherd undertakes before leading his sheep through difficult terrain. A good shepherd never leads his flock where he hasn't first explored. He scouts every path, identifying dangers, and prepares safe passage.

This was a hard reality for me to grasp—or even want to consider—as I grappled to believe God was present when Karissa died. But gently, that reality became an extended branch for me to hold on to.

I offer this same branch to you now—in your darkness: Whatever valley you find yourself in—your Shepherd has already been there. He has studied the terrain, accounted for every hazard, and has prepared the way to walk you *through* it.

One pastor put it this way:

> *"When you wonder where God is in your suffering, remember—He was already here. He was waiting for you in your suffering."* [xii]

I would close my eyes and try to imagine this:

While I was waiting for God to show up in my pain—He was already present. When Jesus allowed Himself to be beaten and spat upon, stripped, humiliated, and crucified, it was His way of saying:

I am here with you—in your suffering.

If Jesus had found a way around suffering, we would expect God to show us a way around our suffering," continues McManus. Our Shepherd-God became human and walked *through* suffering so He could show us the way to walk *through* ours.

It took me a while to grasp those words. I had loved Jesus deeply for more than a decade. That love didn't change, but my assurance of His love *for me* would be something I would wrestle with for months to come. I would need to experience the depths of these truths many times before I could embrace them. So, I kept reaching … and every once in a while, I could feel the strength of His truth leveling the path for me—truths I would continue to learn how to stand on in the years ahead.

Beloved, I pray this steadying grace meets you right where you are.

Because Jesus endured His own dark night of the soul, He is fully qualified to walk with you through yours.

He will not abandon you.

He will not let this destroy you.

He will not leave you in the valley.

He is walking ahead of you. He is walking beside you. He will carry you through.

And you will come out—one day—wounded but not conquered.

CHAPTER 5

AT WORK IN THE DARK

Send me your light and your faithful care,
let them lead me;
let them bring me to your holy mountain,
to the place where you dwell.
Psalm 43:3 (NIV)

Field Trip Object Lessons

Some of my favorite childhood memories are from elementary school field trips—those magical days when textbooks were left behind, and learning happened beyond the classroom. One of the most unforgettable trips was in fourth grade, when our giddy class boarded a bus to explore Rushmore Cave in South Dakota's Black Hills.

Dim bulbs flickered as we descended into the cave, pretending to be brave. Cement stairs led us deep into the belly of the cave. A wooden bridge creaked beneath our feet, making it feel as though we were venturing into the very bowels of the earth.

In my fourth-grade imagination (which has never dimmed), we weren't just on a field trip—we were explorers uncovering an ancient civilization. Sharp stalactites formed a crystal canopy overhead, fueling our sense of wonder. At the cave's lowest point, the guide paused. With a mischievous grin, he informed us there were bats hidden in the walls, emerging only in complete darkness.

Then, he began to count down. Three… Two… One…

And the lights went out. Huddled close to the parent chaperones, the *brave* boys were the first to scream. I might have used it as leverage for years—if I could have resisted joining my peers in the chaos. I doubt an actual bat wing brushed the top of my head, but in the moment, I was *certain* something had grazed it. Real or imagined, it made for an epic story at the dinner table that night.

The guide's voice broke the panic. *"Do you see the shadow of your buddy next to you?"* he asked. We all knew the answer—absolutely not. No matter how long we lingered in the belly of that chilly cave, our eyes would never adjust. Why? Because without a light source, darkness remains absolute.

Before restoring the cave lights, our guide flicked on a small, single-bulb flashlight. A faint beam cut through the blackness, softening it, casting gentle shadows around us. We could vaguely identify our friends. Exhaling in relief, we exchanged sheepish grins with our classmates.

After Karissa's death, I felt like the kid in the inky black cave, wanting to scream for someone to turn on the light. I quoted Psalm 23 daily, trying to summon the courage David seemed to possess. *I will fear no evil in this valley of the shadow of death.*

He didn't deny the presence of evil—but he refused to live in fear of it. I wanted to know how?

How had he learned to trust God's presence, when he couldn't see His face?

I wondered how long it would take before hope turned into experience—before I could feel God's presence with me. David sounded confident. I wasn't sure I would ever reach that place.

Fear no evil?

To be honest, I was paralyzed with fear of it. Evil had devastated my home. My life. It had taken my daughter from my arms. In the darkness of my despair, God felt absent. I was afraid of my own shadow.

Then one day, the long-forgotten lesson from that fourth-grade field trip surfaced: *No shadow exists without a source of light.*

Maybe I had been waiting for God to enter my soul like the noonday sun on a summer day—and in doing so, I was missing the gentle evidence of His presence already appearing in the blackness. Perhaps His shadowy presence was visible in the people who drew near, so I wouldn't be alone. Maybe it showed up in a single promise that would rise unexpectedly and tether me to hope, just enough to find my next breath.

Scripture had said it all along:

In Him (Jesus) *was life,*
and that life was the light of all mankind.
The light shines in the darkness,
and the darkness has not overcome it.
John 1:4-5 (NIV)

Along the journey I discovered, God is not overwhelmed by our darkness. Scripture testifies that He often hides within it to conquer the enemy—using darkness to defeat darkness.

"He made darkness his covering,
his canopy around him, thick clouds dark with water"
Psalm 18:11(ESV)

He shrouded himself in darkness,
veiling his approach with dense rain clouds.
2 Samuel 22:12 (NLT)

David and other psalmists wrote of God's power at work *within* dark circumstances. His presence may not blaze like fire—but His shadow still bears witness: We are not alone.

I once heard the story of a boy trapped in a house fire. His father stood below the two-story window, urging his child to jump. Seeing only a dim shadow through the smoke, the boy cried, *"I can't jump, Daddy. I can't see you."* His father replied, *"That's okay, son. I can see you."* Whether this story is real or an urban legend, its message became so comforting to me:

Even when I couldn't discern God's presence in my pain, He never lost sight of me. As a matter of fact, I now believe He does some of His best work in the dark. Sometimes it's hard to believe that.

As I pondered how we grew in the inky blackness of our mother's womb—fearfully and wonderfully made by the Creator, He helped me recognize that just because I couldn't see God's work, didn't mean it wasn't happening. (See Psalm 139:13-15)

At Work in The Dark

You light a lamp for me.
The LORD, my God, lights up my darkness.
Psalm 18:28 (NLT)

Over the long arc of my own healing, I began to recognize definite markers of God's presence—many of them invisible at the time. What felt hidden then, slowly became something I could name later: God had not left us—even when I couldn't see Him.

Allow me to skip forward several years to illustrate God's faithful work in the darkness of our lives. In the years ahead, I would experience the joy of raising more children. One of them—our third—would walk through a dark chapter of her own.

After graduation, our daughter Kassie spent six months with an organization called Youth with a Mission (YWAM). The program included three months of discipleship training, followed by an overseas ministry trip. A few weeks before her departure to Japan, she called us in tears.

"Mom, Dad, I'm so homesick. I don't think I can endure another couple of months in Japan."

We knew this was more than an emotional low. Of all our children, Kassie thrives on connection—on shared space, shared experiences, shared laughter. This was her first extended separation from our family. As the loneliness settled in—she began spiraling into a deep darkness. Anticipating this, I had already booked a ticket to Kona, planning to spend a few days with her before she left for Japan—just enough time to refuel her soul.

But while packing for the trip, her call came.

Every part of me wanted to say, "*Hang on, I'm coming*". Instead, I felt prompted to let her remain in that tension a little longer, so she might fully receive the joy of what was about to come. So, I told her a special Christmas package was scheduled to arrive the next day—a little something to cheer her up.

My plane landed around 11:00 a.m., just three miles from her school. My phone rang. It was Kassie again—clearly upset.

"Mom, the mail came—but it didn't arrive."

Since I was *the package,* all I could do was listen. I was too close now to ruin the surprise.

"I am going to hang up and call the post office," I said, feigning frustration. "*The tracking number still says it's coming today. I paid good money for that package, so it better be on its way.*"

She informed me she was going to take a nap—unusual for our adventure-loving girl. I knew it was one of those pillow-over-the-head, dark-night-moments. I couldn't reach the campus fast enough.

When I arrived, I explained the plan to the mailroom host. Without hesitation, she joined the conspiracy and called Kassie's room.

"Another delivery just arrived. You have a package ready for pickup."

Kassie said she'd be right down.

Perfect. I handed my camera to my new accomplice and ducked behind the counter, feeling all the butterflies of a momentous surprise. The door opened, and I heard my girl's sweet voice. My heart threatened to burst with compassion.

"Hi, you called about a package?"

"Oh yes," the woman said. "You must be Kassie. Let me grab it for you."

I winked from behind the counter, liquid joy already streaming down my cheeks.

Kassie stepped forward—and I stood up and locked eyes with my precious girl.

She froze—then crumpled to the floor sobbing. I bolted around the barrier and wrapped her in my arms, holding her as though I could pour strength back into her bones.

During our days together, she would randomly say things like, *"Mom, the sky is bluer. The flowers are brighter. The sunshine feels warmer. Even the snow-cones taste better."*

Nothing about her circumstances had changed—except this: she was no longer alone. And that changed everything.

As I watched her breathe again, I felt something surface in me, too.

After Karissa died, I cried out to God so many times, asking, *"Are You listening? Do You see me? Do you care?"*

It would take time before I could say this with any confidence—but eventually I began to see it: God had not forgotten me.

I couldn't have said that in the early days. Back then, it would have sounded impossible. But slowly—almost imperceptibly—I noticed that God was at work within my darkness. I didn't recognize it while I was living it. Only later could I look back and begin to see.

What my soul needed most was already in motion, even when I couldn't sense it. What I feared God was overlooking, He was quietly tending to. The details were already held by God. His timing—so different from mine—was steady, even when my faith wasn't. His goodness wasn't loud, nor did it feel immediate, but it was drawing nearer than I knew.

Scripture later helped me name what I had lived: He gives *treasures—secret riches—hidden in darkness. (See Isaiah 45:3)* Perhaps some of life's rarest gifts are discovered there.

During Job's long season of suffering, he reached for words that still steady me:

"God uncovers mysteries hidden in darkness;
He brings light to deepest gloom."
(Job 12:22 NLT)

Job didn't say the darkness vanished. He spoke these words from inside the abyss of suffering and feelings of utter abandonment—declaring what he knew to be true when he couldn't see it. Over time, I learned that God doesn't abandon us in our heart-wrenching valleys. He meets us there and quietly illumines them—sometimes so gently we only recognize His presence later. Yet, even there, we are not alone.

V. Raymond Edmond once observed, *"Never doubt in the dark what God told you in the light."*[xiii] I understand the wisdom in that now.

But I also know how hard it is to hold onto truth when life feels clear one day and utterly undone the next.

Scripture urges us,

Be strong and courageous.
Do not be afraid or terrified—for the Lord your God goes with you;
He will never leave you nor forsake you.
Deuteronomy 31:6 (NIV)

And yet, when darkness settles in, our hearts often answer back: *You expect me to be strong? Courageous? My world has fallen apart.* In those moments, what was offered as an encouragement, sounds absurd—even an insult to our pain. God can feel distant—even absent.

What I've come to trust is this: God's promises are not undone by shadowed circumstances or the fragility of our faith. Their strength doesn't depend on how steady we feel. Instead, God offers Himself—our quiet Comfort in the dark.

So, what if the darkness itself became a reminder?

The Light may be closer than we think.

CHAPTER 6

THE GOOD SHEPHERD

"I am the good shepherd.
The good shepherd lays down his life for the sheep.
John 10:11 (NIV)

I once read that sheep require more care than any other class of livestock. I don't have much experience with sheep—and I've never met a shepherd—but I *have* witnessed what devoted care looks like.

My sister Karen has been a cattle rancher in South Dakota for decades. She and her late husband, Phil, worked the ranch together for most of their lives. Over time, I came to understand what it meant to live for the well-being of a herd.

Every day, Phil drove the vast stretches of his ranch, checking on his cattle—watching for injury, illness, or danger. Calving season revealed the depth of his devotion. They worked together around the clock, often through cold, sleepless nights, helping struggling heifers deliver their calves. More than once, I watched Phil's entire arm disappear inside a heifer as he repositioned a breech calf. With practiced hands, he secured chains around the tiny legs, and pulled that calf into the world—then, he stitched the mother and stayed until both were safe.

Seeing even one of those moments was enough to convince me real care requires vigilance, caring included dirty hands, and commitment, and that often came at a cost.

It is difficult for me to even imagine a greater level of care and commitment than that. And yet Scripture tells us Jesus is a *better* shepherd—the Great Shepherd who willingly laid down His life for His sheep. (John 10:11 NIV)

Jesus once asked a question to expose the heart of that kind of care:

"If a man has a hundred sheep
and one of them wanders away,
what will he do?
Won't he leave the ninety-nine
others on the hills
and go out to search for the one
that is lost?"
Matthew 18:12 (NLT)

With this simple question, He revealed something tender and incomprehensible at the same time—our irreplaceable worth.

Parents understand this instinctively. If one of your children went missing, you wouldn't hesitate. You would leave the others in safe hands and search until that child was found. Everything else would fade. That child would become your only concern.

Love doesn't calculate the cost. It simply pursues.

This truth came alive for me—not in a pasture, but in a crowd.

In the years that followed Karissa's death, our family slowly grew again. By the time our youngest was still a baby, we found ourselves embarking on our first trip to Disneyland together.

Just outside the gates it looked like half the planet had decided to join us. I dropped to my knees in front of my four little ones, suddenly aware of how one of them could easily be lost. The sea of moving legs towered over them, and the crowds pressed in from every direction.

"Listen carefully," I said, keeping my voice assuring. "If we get separated today, don't go running through the crowd looking for Daddy or me. Sit down on the nearest curb and remind yourself: *Mommy and Daddy love me. Right now, they are coming for me.* We will search until we find you. Nothing else in Disneyland will matter until we are all together again.

They nodded, wide-eyed and trusting.

Healthy parents would never expect a lost and frightened child to find her own way back to them. A mother's world comes to a screeching halt if her child is missing. A father doesn't stop searching until his child is safely in his arms.

That child is you.

That child is me… lost in the 3:00 a.m. dark night of the soul. Sitting quietly on the curb of grief, hoping the Good Shepherd is still looking. That truth steadied me when I could barely steady myself.

Even with my limited understanding of sheep, I know this much: sheep do not search for their shepherd. The shepherd searches for the sheep. We are the focus of our Shepherd's compassion. Nothing matters more to Him than the rescue of our suffering and frightened hearts—that includes yours. He will go to impossible lengths to find *you*—to lift you where you've fallen, to draw you close, no matter how rugged the terrain.

After Karissa's death and burial, I became that terrified child--alone in a crowd, aching in the dark. I wanted to trust God instead of surrendering to fear, but I wondered if He could find me in this hidden place—a girl still holding desperately to truths that once felt solid but now seemed distant and led to so many questions. I wished

I could understand so many things. Why it had happened. What had I done wrong? Why did God's nearness seem absent?

Over long months, that dark place of lostness began to transform into something unexpected. Jesus met me in the shadowlands. He didn't hurry me. He didn't shame me for being stuck with so many questions. I longed to be further along in the grief journey—more trusting and faith-filled. But that wasn't me, and He didn't seem upset by it. He simply wrapped me in His tender, patient kindness and began a slow work of mending my shattered heart.

His Presence became more important to me than anything else. Often my awareness of God's presence didn't last long enough, but it was there when I could notice the beauty in a flower, or smell the loveliness of a fragrance, and hear the joy of a birdsong again. But these were brief glimpses. Sometimes God's presence felt like a glorious sunset that quickly melted away in the encroaching darkness. But then… He would come again, not like afternoon sunshine or the warmth of late spring. Sometimes His appearance felt more like the first light of dawn gently pressing back the night—the realization He had carried me through another brutal memory or a longing for Karissa that cut deep.

However, He comes into your story, He remains *The Place of Presence*—a guide through the darkness and a guardian when you've lost your way. He doesn't demand the absence of fear but simply invites you to come as you are into *The Place* where your fears can subside in a growing awareness of His love.

Beloved, it may take a long time to believe this is true and that's okay: The Father has not lost track of you—not even here, in your darkest night. Right where you are, He offers His gentle companionship, His tender compassion, and His strong hand to steady you until the trembling subsides.

He will illuminate your darkness and whisper with quiet assurance: *You are not alone. I am right here… with you.*

INVITING GOD TO BECOME YOUR PLACE OF PRESENCE

God longs to meet you here—even in the darkness. You might imagine that lost child, sitting still, listening for the familiar sound of a parent's voice calling her name.

If you're able, allow these Scriptures to become small points of light along your path—not demands, just reminders that God is with you, right here, right now. Use the prompts as they serve you, to begin an honest, unhurried conversation with Him.

Wait for the LORD;
be strong and take heart and wait for the LORD.
Psalm 27:14 (NIV)

Acknowledge Your Darkness

Where do you feel most unsure, alone, overwhelmed, or unable to sense God's presence in this darkness?

Remember His Nearness

Read Psalm 139:1–12 slowly, at your own pace. If you can, ask God to show you that there is no place too far from His presence—not the grave, nor the farthest ocean, not even your deepest night.

O LORD, you have examined my heart
and know everything about me.
You know when I sit down or stand up.
You know my thoughts even when I'm far away.

You see me when I travel
and when I rest at home.
You know everything I do.
You know what I am going to say
even before I say it, Lord*.*
You go before me and follow me.
You place your hand of blessing on my head.
Such knowledge is too wonderful for me,
too great for me to understand!

I can never escape from your Spirit!
I can never get away from your presence!
If I go up to heaven, you are there;
if I go down to the grave, you are there.

If I ride the wings of the morning,
if I dwell by the farthest oceans,
even there your hand will guide me,
and your strength will support me.
I could ask the darkness to hide me
and the light around me to become night—
but even in darkness I cannot hide from you.
To you the night shines as bright as day.
Darkness and light are the same to you.
Psalm 139:1-12 (NLT)

Have there been moments—even faint ones—when God's nearness felt possible or present?

Receive His Invitation

Read Psalm 130. It describes a soul waiting with deep ache but deeper hope. God is not asking you to pretend the night is bright. He is gently inviting you—at your own pace—to trust that morning is coming.

Out of the depths I call to you, Lord!
Lord, listen to my voice;
let your ears be attentive
to my cry for help.
I wait for the Lord;
I wait
and put my hope in his word.
I wait for the Lord
more than watchmen for the morning—
more than watchmen for the morning.
Israel, put your hope in the Lord.
For there is faithful love with the Lord,
and with him is redemption in abundance.
Psalm 130:1-2, 5-7 (NIV)

What might God be gently inviting me toward today—if anything?

Root Yourself in Scripture

Read these three passages again—aloud if that feels helpful. Notice if a word, phrase, or image quietly lingers with you.

Respond Honestly

Bring your honest fears, doubts, and longings before Him. He is listening. He is speaking.

My prayer in this place of waiting:

Prayer on the Dark Path

Oh Father, I long for You. I need the assurance that You are near. Please reveal Yourself to me in my darkness. When I cannot see Your face, help me trust that Your hands are still at work. Help me discover the treasure of Your steadfast love and tender care.

Good Shepherd. I wait for You. My soul cries out with the prophet: "I will never forget this awful time as I grieve over my loss.

Yet, I still dare to hope when I remember this:
The faithful love of the Lord never ends.
His mercies never cease.
Great is His faithfulness;
His mercies begin fresh each morning.
I say to myself, the Lord is my inheritance,
therefore, I will hope in Him."
Lamentations 3:20-24 (NLT)

Amen.

SECTION THREE

The Place of Peace

For All My Anxiety

Now may the Lord of peace himself
give you peace at all times
and in every way.

2 Thessalonians 3:16 NIV

CHAPTER 7

BE STILL AND KNOW

"Be still, and know that I am God..."
Psalm 46:10a (NIV)

Tug of War

I have never been known as an anxious person, but grief has a way of stirring up emotions you didn't know were hidden. One of my earliest brushes with anxiety came as a child, during those tense minutes before the recess bell rang—when the teacher announced it was group sports day. I was a confident kid. I had good friends, did well in school, and was already finding my way as a budding musician.

But that confidence crumbled on the playground. Two kids were selected as captains, tasked with assembling their dream teams. With each new pick, the chosen players huddled and whispered advice about who should be added. The longer I stood there, I began wondering who had come up with this selection process and how it remained the best option for team selection? Fragile hearts were being formed...and while I didn't think mine was fragile...this certainly wasn't helping! Did anyone really believe ten-year-old kids held the capacity to choose fairly? From my vantage point, it was an awful strategy.

Week after week, it was always the same scenario. *Here we go again.* I braced myself for another round of humiliation as teams were selected. My heart raced. My face reddened. I forced myself to appear aloof, knowing eye contact with the captains would betray my desperation. The ever-thinning options eroded any remaining trace of dignity.

Then came the weekly battle:

You can have her.

Nope, it's your turn to take her. We had her last week.

If it had come down to me and a potted plant beside me, I'm certain they would have picked the plant.

After Karissa's death, anxiety and peace felt a bit like that: opposing teams in a relentless game of tug-of-war. Once again, I wasn't invited onto either team. This time, I was the rope in a fight for my soul. I wondered if I might snap in the battle. While I read scriptures of God's promised peace, it often felt like anxiety was winning the battle.

Memories lingered in the worst places. Anxiety choked the hope of a brighter tomorrow. Explanations from well-meaning individuals, though wrapped in good intentions, yanked hard against the peace I ached for.

"Jesus must have needed her more than you did."
"Heaven gained another angel."
"Who knows how hard life may have turned out for her."
"God must think so highly of you to entrust you with such deep pain."
"At least you're young—you can have another child."
"This suffering will make you stronger."
"It's going to work out. Don't worry, you'll feel better soon."

Perhaps you have experienced the pain of well-intended words—or even offered a comparable sentiment in a desire to help. Most statements are spoken from a heart of genuine love. Suffering unsettles all of us. We long to fix the pain that God may be inviting us to simply hold—to offer our presence over easy answers. I learned—often the hard way—that shallow and hurried sentimentalities can intensify the anguish of a soul already stretched thin.

Years later, author Ann Voskamp would write, "*The places where we are torn to pieces can become thin places where we touch the peace of God.*"[xiv] Those words mean so much to me because I knew how it felt to be torn to pieces. I slowly came to recognize their truth. Those times of stretching, those 'thin places' became *The Place* where God invited me near. *The Place* where His peace enveloped me. Yet stepping into that peace did not come easily. Pain often tempts us to run, to look for quick escapes or easy answers. But God's invitation is different. His invitation is not to flee the storm—but to be still within it. That invitation felt impossible.

Be Still and Know That I Am God

We rarely make our best decisions in the clamor of a storm. Catastrophe stirs up a frantic desire to avoid anything that might worsen our overwhelming pain. For Gary and me that included the place we called home—and at times, even each other.

We leaned heavily on the wisdom of friends who stood outside the vortex of our chaos. Though their counsel often collided with our aching desires, we chose to trust their wisdom. They advised us to be still, to resist making life-altering decisions while navigating the heavy fog of grief. They warned us that tragedy can lure people from jobs, and hearts from marriages—choices that often birth deep regret once the dust settles and the ground steadies.

I understood the enticement of running away, wondering if a fresh start—somewhere new, or even with someone new—could somehow loosen the chokehold of our loss. Friends and family humbly helped us see the deception woven into those imaginations and helped us face our reality.

While our storm involved the loss of a child, many factors can incite this all-consuming grief. Maybe you are facing a life-threatening diagnosis, or the impending loss of someone you love. Perhaps you've spent years battling infertility or enduring miscarriages… and you're exhausted from hiding your grief at yet another baby shower. A job loss may have uprooted your life and separated you from your support system. These experiences, though unique in shape, threaten to crush us under their weight.

What I discovered—slowly… and not without resistance—was that peace did not come by escaping these harsh realities, but by learning to face them. Every attempt to outrun our pain—and the anxiety it produced—only seemed to hinder God's entry into it.

Chasing light when darkness is closing in is like running after the setting sun. The only way to reach morning is to head the other direction—plunging into the darkness until we arrive at the sunrise.

I prayed for the counterintuitive courage Jerry Sittser describes in *A Grace Disguised*—the courage to stop running from grief and instead walk into it, allowing suffering to become a journey of transformation rather than something to escape.[xv]

Initially, I wasn't that brave. Gary and I were desperate to live in God's peace, but it took me a while before I could agree with the thought of facing the brutality of our pain. I longed to outrun it. But eventually, we decided to try to face our pain and stand together on that path, no matter how brutal the journey became. Instead of abandoning one another, we asked God's Spirit to weave the frayed edges of our souls together onto the loom of His indestructible love.

Immediately following Karissa's passing, we spent several days cradled in the quiet shelter of our pastor's home. Part of facing our pain meant recognizing when it was time —time to return to our home. Time to step across the threshold of what once was so dear—and yet would never be the same. I had not stepped inside it since the day the ambulance carried Karissa from our home. That four-mile stretch of road between our pastor's house and ours offered just enough space for doubt to creep in… just enough time to cause us to second-guess our readiness.

As we pulled onto our street, I felt like a motorcycle stuntman suspended mid-air over a canyon of loss. Turning back wasn't an option. A safe landing? Unlikely. Adrenaline rushed like a current under my skin. Had we made a terrible mistake? Our sweet home, once brimming with dreams and laughter, felt like a familiar but distant memory. Now the walls stood silent, watching. This barren land felt like an unlikely place for peace to take root.

Within those walls, healing was neither swift nor steady—more like waves breaking against jagged rocks. The aching hollow left by Karissa's absence was inescapable. Anxiety rose like the tide. The layout of our home demanded I pass her empty nursery several times a day. My chest tightened. My legs faltered. Dread waited like a phantom lurking in the hallway.

Days without sleep left me weary and unraveling. Eventually, Gary contacted my doctor, who prescribed anti-anxiety medication. It promised rest but accepting it brought its own inner conflict. It felt intrusive—like a betrayal of faith, bullying my belief that God was enough. I feared it revealed a threadbare trust. Yet, without it I couldn't hold a cup of tea or a simple conversation.

By day, doubt murmured. By night, it gathered into a clamor. *Were we naïve to think healing could unfold in the very space where our joy had shattered? Was the advice we followed flawed?* But somewhere beneath the noise, a gentler Voice rose—quiet, persistent. What if our weakness was the soil where Divine Peace could grow? In the ache of surrender, a fragile hope unfurled: Maybe—even here, even now—Jesus could find us.

In those splintered days of early grief, God allowed Gary and me to confront the limitations of our humanity. We recognized our frailty and, in humility, admitted our need for medical help, our need for others, and ultimately—our need for Him. Though self-accusing voices continued to belittle us, Gary and I refused to finish the song that shame started. We turned down its volume by trying to exercise gratitude and thanksgiving—gratitude for the wisdom of others. Gratitude for medicine that could steady an unraveling soul. These, too, became gifts of grace—helping people like us walk *through* sorrow, not around it.

Each night before bed, we prayed for each other's minds—two weary souls clinging to God. We would break the anti-anxiety pill in half, offering it to one another like communion. A shared surrender. Together, we invited the Holy Spirit into those long nights, asking Him to gather up our scattered, regretful thoughts and guide our dreams onto pathways of peace—and even joy.

And He answered—sometimes slowly, sometimes unevenly—one would lay awake while the other dozed. But still--He began to give us rest—a glorious, undeserved gift—for our bodies and our minds.

As I peered through the gaping holes of my inadequacy, I discovered I wasn't alone in this mess. Within the uncomfortable tangle of doubt, fear, and grief, I became aware of God's nearness. I began to notice new dimensions of His nature. His strong hand enveloping mine—the only hand capable of lifting me out of the crippling chaos and offering me the firm footing of His peace.

The great pastor, Charles Spurgeon, once wrote of his own suffering, *"I have looked back to times of trial with a kind of longing, not to have them return, but to feel the strength of God as I have felt it then, to feel the power of faith, as I have felt it then, to hang upon God's powerful arm as I hung upon it then, and to see God at work as I saw him then."*[xvi]

In our weakness, we would find something we never could have grasped in strength—a nearness to God we didn't know we lacked, and a peace we never thought possible. It didn't happen overnight. It was a long journey. We were living a story we would have never written, yet God was meeting us in every line.

We didn't have answers. We didn't have certainty. But we had Him. And somehow, in that hard-fought, quiet place of surrender, He became enough.

CHAPTER 8

86,400 MOMENTS OF GRACE

As a father has compassion on his children,
so the LORD has compassion on those who fear him;
for he knows how we are formed,
he remembers that we are dust.
Psalm 103:13-14 (NIV)

Shifting The Atmosphere

Grief often awakens the soul before the body stirs. Sometimes the agonizing sobs rise before the sun, before the alarm has its say. Another day breaks, and the ache remains—relentless, waiting. I whisper into the silence, "*Will I remain here forever, an exile wandering in this wilderness of sorrow?*"

Yet, Lamentations—written from the ashes—sowed different words into desolate ground like mine.

Because of the Lord's faithful love
we do not perish,
for His mercies never end.
They are new every morning;
great is Your faithfulness!
Lamentations 3:22-23 (CSB)

I didn't feel those words at first. I only wondered when it would be true for me—that every morning would carry not only light, but mercy. That the rising sun would become a divine invitation into something new. That perhaps this wilderness would no longer feel like punishment—but *The Place* where God revealed Himself in ways I hadn't known.

Nothing about our circumstances had changed. Our address was the same. Our grief was still heavy. And yet—slowly—something in the atmosphere began to shift.

I noticed it one morning before the faint light of dawn. Gary had queued soft music in our bedroom before leaving for work. Instead of waking to the familiar weight of anguish, I was stirred by lyrics—gentle and steadying—declaring God's nearness, affirming His steadfast love, His dominion over darkness—His vast Power at work on my behalf.

Tears came. These were not the acid tears of despair, but something more tender—like rain falling on parched ground. Worship was becoming an invitation into communion with God. God used these songs to remind me of His unfailing love. Truth began to interrupt the enemy's attempts to root turmoil in my mind. Gradually, in ways I couldn't predict or control, peace began to replace the fear of waking to another morning. I sensed Jesus near, whispering what I could not always feel: *You are not alone. I am your peace.*

Music has always held the power. Before David ever wore a crown, he was summoned to King Saul's troubled palace—not to advise, but to play music. When Saul's spirit was tormented, David's harp brought calm. The shadows in King Saul's mind would retreat. The atmosphere changed—not through strategies, but through song—turning chaos into stillness.

I've noticed how music does this—it finds a way to slip past the intellect, disarming the soul. Recording artist, Michael Card reflects, *"Socrates once said, 'When the soul hears music, it drops its best guard'. Music can open a door in the heart of the listener and beautify the interior of that soul. Music anchors our belief in what we are singing about. How many times, in the midst of worry or grief, has a song lifted you out of that dark place and left you in another better place, a place with more light and air?"*

Gary chose songs that felt like love letters from heaven—many woven with the ancient language of the Psalms. Declarations from God's word filled the hollow places of my soul. I breathed them in like oxygen—not to force peace to come, but to make room for it. Inhaling truth. Exhaling fear.

The worship didn't just shift something in the room—it began to shift something in me. It dismantled the heavy shroud that clung to my thoughts. It began opening doors within me, previously shut tight. Light was allowed to enter where it had been dark for too long.

I was re-awakening to God's unimpaired love. Lyrics gave language to my soul, vacant of words. They become the voice of my longing when I couldn't identify it.

David once wrote:

Hearken unto the voice of my cry, my King, and my God:
for unto thee will I pray.
My voice shalt thou hear in the morning,
O Lord in the morning will I direct my prayer
unto thee and will look up.
Psalm 5 (KJV)

These were lyrics penned by David—they were not triumphant declarations. They were not simply prayers, saved for desperate days. They were prayers of decision—the choice to turn toward God before the day turned on him. Those words were becoming mine, too. Before my feet touched the floor, I would whisper, '*God, I look to You. Before I face the ache, before I face the silence, I will direct my cry upward. Even when I can't find my voice—and can't feel what I know to be true'*.

The intimacy of first-person lyrics—not *about* God but *to* God—deepened my hunger for His presence. He was entering my heart as *The Place* of indescribable peace hovering over me, the footing beneath me, the fortress surrounding me, the ointment soothing the searing pain within. Every cell in my body cried out for more of Him. I allowed the torrent of tears to flow—each one caught in His nail-scarred hands—and transformed by His love.

Sometimes I felt those pierced hands hover over me, transforming my tears into healing rain. Like water finding the grooves carved by sorrow, Jesus' peace flowed into every pain-gouged trench—a sacred stream of Living Water, washing me whole.

The mornings were more than a moment tethered to a particular song—they were thresholds into discovering a deeper kind of peace, not bound by time or a feeling. Even as melodies faded and mornings gave way to long days, I was learning this truth: peace wasn't limited to a song at sunrise—it was in a Person, present in every breath, in all the silence, in the returning—again and again.

Fixed

You will keep in perfect peace
all who trust in you,
all whose thoughts are fixed on you!
Isaiah 26:3 (NLT)

Unlike medicine, peace isn't rationed or measured out. It isn't earned by effort or consistency. It is received through relationship. Sometimes that looked like clinging to a single line of Scripture over breakfast. Other days, when dread hovered like a storm cloud, it looked like stepping outside and whispering, *"I know You are near."*

I began writing verses on sticky notes and placing them in spots where my eyes would land when fear tried to take over. These weren't cures, but they felt like anchors. I would talk to God about them—recording thoughts in my journal—wrestling with the gap between His unfailing promises and my less-than-promising reality.

These were honest conversations with Jesus, where He slowly filled the empty and ordinary spaces of my day with His presence. My thoughts—often hijacked by fear and fragmented by grief—would settle, if only briefly, into the truth of who God is—a Father, who promises to never leave or forsake us.

When facing your own day feels as daunting as facing a giant, God doesn't rush us forward. He meets us in the 86,400 seconds of a day—sometimes unseen, sometimes unexpectedly—carrying us through one moment and accompanying us into the next.

His peace didn't magically erase my grief. But it shifted the atmosphere of my soul—from panic to becoming present with Him, from anguish to amazement that He would stay in the mess. He was willing to carry the weight of my sorrow on His shoulders, while He wrapped His peace around mine.

But you, God, see the trouble of the afflicted;
you consider their grief and take it in hand.
Psalm 10:14a (NIV)

If you are a weary sojourner, can you offer Him your pain? God sees your grief. He will hold it with the utmost care.

Peace is not a demand to feel better. The truth is, some of us may not be ready to find peace or joy or reprieve because we fear it would separate us from the truth of something that was lost.

Peace is simply an invitation to be held in this brutal tangle of pain. Jesus isn't offering you a better emotion to navigate grief. Jesus is offering Himself—*The Prince of Peace.*

Whenever you turn toward Him—even falteringly—you are turning toward the Source who longs to mend your shattered heart.

He was becoming A Refuge for my mornings. A Shelter as I walked past Karissa's room. A Steadying Presence when anxiety threatened to undo me. I didn't wake up healed. But I genuinely felt held in the arms of Peace.

Do not worry about anything.
Instead pray about everything,
and the peace of God that transcends all understanding
will guard your mind in Christ Jesus.
Philippians 4:6-7 (NLT)

His peace is beyond our ability to understand or to explain—therefore, it must be experienced—and often that comes slowly.

When we're ready, His invitation will stand:

"Come to me, all you who are weary and burdened, and I will give you rest. Take my yoke upon you and learn from me, for I am gentle and humble in heart, and you will find rest for your souls."
Matthew 11:28-29 (NIV)

We don't often use the imagery of a yoke. I've only seen one on the wall in my friend's bedroom. A yoke was a handcrafted tool—shaped to fit across the shoulders of two animals (usually oxen), linking them side by side. It didn't bruise or burden them. In earlier times, a young ox was often yoked beside a stronger, more experienced one—not to pull the weight alone, but to share the weight and learn how to move forward by staying connected to the seasoned ox.

Jesus offers us this kind of yoke and Himself as our steady companion. His yoke isn't forced upon us but gently extended. It doesn't increase our burden—it lifts it. When we accept it, we find ourselves tethered to grace. He teaches us how to rest—not by removing the load, but by carrying it with us.

Grief days continued to bulge with anxiety and so many unanswered questions. The future held so much uncertainty. But I had Him. And in walking beside Him—one unsteady moment at a time, through tears and in the quiet—*The Place of Peace* became my one constant comfort.

CHAPTER 9

LORD, HELP!

Has the LORD redeemed you?
Then speak out!
Psalm 107:2a (NLT)

In my journey through grief, Jesus used concerned friends to lighten my load. They often asked, *"Patty, how can we help? Let us know what you need."* I usually met their kindness with a blank stare and a hesitant shrug. Grief changed shape by the hour. What I needed one moment dissolved in the next. I struggled to find words to share what I couldn't name—to Jesus or to those who longed to help.

Somehow, Psalm 107 reached me in that fog. It became a well-worn place I returned to often. The psalm paints portraits of people lost in varying ways; and testified of one Savior who works on behalf of each person—in sin, suffering, pride, rebellion, foolishness and tragedy: He led them home and satisfied their souls with good things. He broke through walls of iron and gates of bronze to set them free. To those suffering the effects of sin, He healed them. To the ones caught unexpectedly in tragedy, He calmed the storm to a whisper and led them to a safe harbor. They were people, like you and me, who were unsure how to pray. Each story crescendos to the same cry—simple, raw, and timeless:

"Lord, help!"

That was it. No fluffy adjectives. No excuses or suggestions on how God might provide what they needed. Just a guttural cry for mercy—and the hope that He could make sense of all the unspoken words. I found relief—and still do—in these urgent prayers of people like you and me.

Hundreds of years later, Jesus was resting in a boat with His disciples on the Sea of Galilee when a sudden storm swept in without warning. Their cry wasn't polished or poetic—but it was raw, real, and desperate:

The disciples woke Jesus up, shouting,
"Teacher, don't you care that we're going to drown?"
When Jesus woke up, he rebuked the wind
and said to the waves, "Silence! Be still!"
Suddenly the wind stopped,
And there was a great calm. (Mark 4:38b-39b NLT)

Jesus didn't hesitate to respond to their panicked plea—even though it came laced with more than a hint of accusation. To be fair, they were terrified; and let's be honest, few of us get our words right in the thick of fear. These were men who walked with Jesus daily, who witnessed miracles firsthand—yet in that moment, they asked the question I shouted in my storm. Maybe you've whispered something like that too—quietly, or angrily, or barely at all.

Don't You care?

The truth is, if Jesus didn't act, they were goners, and chances are, you've felt the same way. The threat feels real. Your boat is taking on water. You feel moments away from slipping beneath the surface of sorrow. Unwelcome questions rise to the surface and gnaw at you. You try to silence them, beat them down—but they reveal a tremble beneath your faith.

As the waters sweep over us, knocking us off our feet, our tendency is to question, not just His presence—but His care.

I learned firsthand that peace is not the absence of chaos. It is the nearness of God at the heart of it. I came to trust this, even when it was hard to feel: He was with me in the boat.

Peace. Be still.

In His final words to the disciples, Jesus reminded them—and us—that we will never face a storm He is not in the midst of:

> *"I am with you always. Even to the ends of the age."*
> (Matthew 28:20b NLT)

Even here. Even now.

The storm beating against your life is not just something to survive—it's an invitation to witness Jesus' power over it. He responds to your desperate, unpolished cries for help. Whether you feel lost, burdened by despair, reeling from the consequences of someone else's choices, or grappling with regret from your own, Jesus responds with compassion.

He is the Prince of Peace—the One who still calms storms to a whisper and steadies the waves when we cry out to Him (see Psalm 107:27-29). His faithful love becomes visible to those witnessing our chaos (see Psalm 107:43b).

Looking back, I can see that fixed in the center of my storm was an opportunity to encounter God's powerful peace. Those prayers—raw and real—were preserved in Scripture to remind us: God doesn't respond to our word count or word choice. It's not *how* we say it. It's *that* we say it. It is not our polish, but our pain, that bends His ear. And when we cry out—He gives us what we need most: Himself.

Sometimes He quieted the storm; other times, He quieted my soul within it.

Perhaps all you can do right now is whisper, “HELP!” That’s all the Prince of Peace needs to hear.

If all you can do is lean—just a little—toward the Prince of Peace, that is enough.

The Lord will fight for you; you need only to be still.
Exodus 14:14 (NIV)

How Shall I Pray?

In one of my favorite books of poetry, *Guerrillas of Grace,* Ted Loder offers a collection of poetic prayers for life’s many seasons. They spoke to the questions I faced in those moments when words became tangled inside me—when pain swelled beyond articulation.

Maybe like me, you’ve wondered whether Jesus could make sense of the prayers you cannot fully form? Sometimes all I had to offer Him were tears. Did those count? At other times, it was simply the opening up of my trembled hands—or groans and sighs rising from somewhere deep within.

My prayers weren’t pretty. I had no fragrant flowers or polished praises to offer Him–only a messy mixture of tainted trust and fragile faith.

But somehow, I felt that even those disordered prayers mattered to God. Perhaps that was because of what I saw repeatedly in Scripture:

In Psalm 40, David writes, *“I waited patiently for the Lord; he turned to me and heard my cry.”*

No harp in hand. No melody to soften his anguish. Just a cry for help—and God turns toward it, receiving it as a prayer. David stands with all who suffer, offering nothing manicured or rehearsed—only raw need.

Like David, we will face circumstances that squeeze a desperate cry from the depths of our souls. When I couldn't arrange words, my journal bore the weight of my sorrow—words without arrangement.

Page after page absorbed the ink of scrambled thoughts… undaunted trust interrupted by torrents of pain. I am convinced God received every word and phrase. He entered the ragged landscape of my soul to become *My Place of Peace.*

"He lifted me out of the slimy pit, out of the mud and mire. He set my feet on a rock and gave me a firm place to stand."
Psalm 40:2 (NIV)

God invites us to place our weight on His Word. He declares,

"I have sworn by my own name.
I have spoken the Truth and will never go back on My Word."
Isaiah 45:23 (NLT)

In one of those moments, I made a quiet choice to trust Him—to cast all the anxieties of that moment on the One who truly cared (1 Peter 5:7). Though He knew I would continue to wrestle between trust and doubt, He met me in that moment, filling the cracks in my faith with His sustaining grace.

He has grace for the gaps in your faith, too. He desires to be a steady foundation beneath you. Peace—even while you're simply learning to stand.

Circumstances may try to accuse God of abandonment. But He is not threatened by those accusations, nor repulsed by our messy, anxious hearts. His love is unwavering.

Peace may come in fragments, in borrowed strength, or you may not feel it at all for a while. That doesn't mean God is absent. And it doesn't mean you are doing anything wrong. Peace is not something *you* achieve—it is Someone who draws near.

I often wondered if anyone had felt as lost on their journey as I did. I thought I would be further down the trail—that my emotions would be steadier by now. As I look in the rearview mirror, I would reassure my younger self—and anyone who finds herself on a similar path: Be encouraged. You are not behind. You are not failing. You are being held.

Into your fiercest storm, I pray you hear Jesus, whispering:

"*Even here—I am with you. Peace. Be still.*"

INVITING GOD TO BECOME YOUR PLACE OF PEACE

Be still and know that I am God.
Psalm 46:10a

Do you have a favorite spot—a comfortable place to pause for a moment? In this quiet space, give yourself permission to stop striving, even briefly. You don't have to try to calm your thoughts or fix what feels tangled. You are simply invited to pause.

Take a deep breath in. Let it out slowly.

God knows you. He sees you. You are safe here—free from all judgment and expectation in *The Place of Peace.*

Jesus is nearer than you may feel. He hears the ache you find difficult to express.

You might begin by simply admitting: *"Jesus, I don't even know how to pray right now."*

That is enough.

These simple prompts help you begin a conversation with Jesus.

You don't need to answer every question. You may choose one—or come up with your own.

1. *In what ways have I felt the urge to outrun my pain—simply because it felt too heavy to face?*
2. *What is the storm I'm facing right now? I name it—not to give it power, but to invite Jesus into it.*

3. *Have there been moments—however small—when I sensed God's faithfulness in past storms? How might remembering those moments steady me now?*

4. *What desperate or unpolished prayers have I wanted to say? Am I willing to offer them to Jesus, trusting that my pain—not my perfection—moves His heart?*

The following promises from God's Word have been prayed over you. As you read, listen for a word or phrase that feels meaningful to you—there is no need to rush.

Though the mountains be shaken and the hills be removed,
yet my unfailing love for you will not be shaken
nor my covenant of peace be removed,"
says the LORD, who has compassion on you.
Isaiah 54:10 (NIV)

Cast all your anxiety on him because he cares for you.
1 Peter 5:7 (NIV)

The Lord gives strength to his people;
the Lord blesses his people with peace.
Psalm 29:11

Don't fret or worry. Instead of worrying, pray. Let petitions and praises shape your worries into prayers, letting God know your concerns. Before you know it, a sense of God's wholeness, everything coming together for good, will come and settle you down. It's wonderful what happens when Christ displaces worry at the center of your life.
Philippians 4:6-7 The Message (MSG)

- Is the Holy Spirit causing anything to resonate in your heart right now?
- In light of what stood out, share your feelings with Jesus. This is the essence of prayer.

- If it's helpful, you may record your prayer.
- Consider displaying meaningful scriptures somewhere you can easily see them when anxiety creeps in. In the midst of the chaos, scripture holds the power to interrupt the spiral. Peace rarely replaces panic all at once—but even small shifts can become a gift that incrementally grows over time.
- As you return to God's promises, how might God's peace replace your panic?"

A Prayer for Your Anxious Heart

Lord, I come to You—not with answers, but with ache.
I feel the storm.
I feel the ache of loss… the weight of what I cannot fix… the fear of what comes next.

Sometimes I wonder if You see me—if You care.
Like the disciples, I cry out:
"Don't You care that I'm drowning?"

But here I am, Lord.
Still reaching.
Still hoping You're in the boat.
Still trusting that You're the God who calms storms with a word—and meets me in the middle of mine.

So, I offer my clenched hands.
My racing thoughts.
My anxious heart.

Calm the storm within me, Lord.
Speak Your words of peace over my fear:
Peace. Be still.

I trust You with what I can't untangle.
Thank You for receiving my mess as prayer.
Thank You for staying with me in this storm.
Amen.

SECTION FOUR

The Place of Provision

For All My Emptiness

Let your face smile on us, Lord.
You have given me greater joy
than those who have abundant
harvests of grain and new wine.

Psalm 4:6b-7 NLT

CHAPTER 10

WHEN EMPTY HANDS ARE ENOUGH

Open wide your mouth and I will fill it.
Psalm 81:10b – NIV

A Sculpture of Suffering

We attended our first marriage retreat just five weeks after Karissa's death. Many of our friends filled the large room—hands intertwined, wives snuggling close to husbands, eyes bright with anticipation. This was a rare weekend without children, a chance to focus on each other.

Gary and I arrived with far less hope and none of the enthusiasm. We clung to each other—not out of romance, but survival. Our goal was to simply keep the other from falling apart. We felt like dry twigs in air pregnant with expectancy, afraid our sorrow might puncture the mood at any given moment. The grooves of agony etched into our faces betrayed our brave attempts to hide our fractured hearts.

The session opened in worship, a doorway into the shelter of God's presence. This was where I longed to linger. Here, I was sheltered from well-meaning comments. In this space, I didn't have to dam the easy flow of tears. We were grateful for friends whose compassion had surrounded us. But this weekend… they needed to focus on each other—on their marriages. They needed a break from our grief as much as we did.

The speaker launched the weekend with an activity: each participant was given a small piece of molding clay and asked to create a sculpture that reflected the current state of their soul. Normally, I would have welcomed a creative project, but I had no desire to expose the raw condition of my soul. I had hoped the weekend might offer a reprieve from its festering pit.

Around the room, while friends erupted in laughter, I felt sweat trickle down my back. This mound of clay described my state, a lump void of beauty or design. It remained untouched in my palms until I worried my inactivity was drawing the very attention I hoped to avoid. I pulled the clump from the bag and began rolling it between my hands.

Surprisingly, the cool clay brought comfort. I loved how it softened to my touch. Slowly, I molded a fragile girl—long, skinny arms dangling at her sides, oversized palms facing forward—magnifying their emptiness. Without Karissa, I had no idea what to do with long days, limp arms, and empty hands.

The speaker walked around the room, asking each person to share the story behind their sculpture. When it was my turn, I offered a brief but honest confession. "*My arms hang limp. Only God can lift them. My hands are empty. Only He can fill them.*"

Pop! *Way to suck the air out of the room, Patty.*

I recognized how life began to lack meaning as emptiness settled into my soul. A deep hunger developed that nothing satisfied for long.

Author Nicole Johnson once compared our souls to Swiss cheese—the holes are evidence that we live in a sin-scarred world.[xvii] They represent longings that ache to be filled. Acknowledging them isn't selfish, though our attempts to fill them often are. We reach for relationships, prestige, or possessions to ease the ache—but nothing apart from God can satisfy.

I had so many longings—I ached for my daughter, for the joy of motherhood, for the life we had before the tragedy. Acknowledging these longings wasn't sinful, but I wasn't sure what to do with them. All I knew was they kept drawing me back to God.

Maybe that's the purpose of longings—to draw us to God—our *Place of Provision.* He knows exactly what's needed for every kind of emptiness. Scripture invites us to come to God empty-handed. For those who have nothing to offer but broken lives and busted stories, this is good news. He opens the way, welcoming us fully into His presence.

So, let us come boldly to the throne of our gracious God.
There we will receive his mercy,
and we will find grace to help us when we need it most.
Hebrews 4:16 (NLT)

God is the Father whose office door is always open. His phone is never silenced. He isn't bothered or annoyed by our constant interruptions. On the contrary, His face lights up when He hears our footsteps. He turns toward us, arms open, offering extravagant mercy and grace as we tramp through His door—carrying nothing but a threadbare sack of broken dreams and misshaped longings.

When a Load of Apples Changes Everything

Five years prior to that retreat, God met me as *The Place of Provision* in college. As the youngest of six children, my parents couldn't afford to contribute much to my education. But I wasn't ready to let go of the dream. I chased every creative avenue—music competitions, pageants, and scholarships—enough to cover my entire freshman year. After that, I waitressed about twenty-five hours a week to fund the rest.

A deep sense of calling fueled my motivation, but my long restaurant shifts still weren't enough. During my sophomore year, the financial pressure became overwhelming. The sweet, middle-aged bursar called me in to discuss my future. If I planned to continue at this private university, I needed to come up with $3,500 within two weeks. She reminded me about student loan options. I gently reminded her that loans were not an option.

My education was preparation for full-time ministry. Before college, I had promised God I would work hard and trust Him to provide. I clung to the mantra: *"If it's God's will, it's God's bill.*"

Each week, I made my way to the finance office, carrying stacks of dollar bills and rolled coins. They counted it, updated my balance, and sent me on my way. I was inching forward—$250 to $300 a week. But deep down, I knew I was incapable of closing the gap. This path was becoming impossibly out of reach.

At nineteen, I had never woken up exhausted—until now. An empty wallet has a way of emptying one's hope. The weight of this financial reality pressed hard. Each new day overwhelmed me before it even began. The pace that once energized me now became a crushing load.

Morning after morning, I carried my heavy heart up a narrow flight of stairs to a small room on campus known as 'The Prayer Tower'. The circular tower overlooked the campus and a sprawling plum orchard. This upper room was completely bare… not even a simple, folding chair. I often found myself face-down before God on that worn-out, turquoise carpet.

It was the only place on campus where I could pour out the full contents of my heart before God. There, He met me. His Word whispered courage into my soul. He patiently unraveled the confusing knot of my thoughts and helped me surrender to His goodness. I usually walked away from these moments a bit taller and lighter, after unloading the weight of all I couldn't control, but lately I had struggled with the reality of releasing the dream of earning my pastoral degree.

Throughout Scripture, individuals used various names to describe God's nature; one of those names is Jehovah Jireh, the Lord who provides. That name had always been dear to me. I gave my life to Him as a child, and over the years, I had learned to run to Him, believing every need—from the sparrow-small concerns to eternal-destiny decisions—mattered deeply to God.

Now that my education was on the brink of ruin, I was wavering between doubt and trust. The prospect of leaving school crushed me, but I had learned to trust God's involvement over every detail of my life. I had to believe I was a story still being written. Maybe the timeline for earning a degree would stretch out longer than I hoped. Maybe the road would look different from what I imagined. But scripture promised, *"The Lord will fulfill His purpose for me." (Psalm 138:8).* I refused to let this financial giant shrink my confidence in God's involvement in my story.

Bethel Pastor, Bill Johnson, once said, *"Faith doesn't deny a problem's existence. It denies it a place of influence."*[xviii] That morning in the prayer tower, I shared the problem: my waitressing job wasn't enough to meet this need. Then I reminded my soul that my job wasn't my provider: He was. He saw the situation. He knew I needed a miracle.

Didn't He say, '*Give all your worries and cares to God, for he cares about you.*' (*1 Peter 5:7 NLT)* If it was true—which I knew it was—then my need mattered. I laid my heavy burden at His feet that morning and left it there. I was out of options.

The two-week deadline flew by. "*Patty O'Grady, please make your way to the finance office.*" My name hung over the cafeteria like a cloud without wind. I was among a small band of students whose education hung in the balance. My financial situation demanded a decision.

I longed to disappear beneath the lunch tables to hide from my carefree peers. I was a straight-A student without the means to continue the education I loved. As I passed a couple of close friends, their eyes appealed to my faltering hope. *"God's got this."*

I took a deep breath, reminding myself of what I so boldly declared in the prayer room. Had I approached God like a genie in a bottle, expecting Him to rescue me with a cash envelope under my pillow or a miraculous tip tucked beneath a customer's plate? I quietly repented of any entitled expectations I had placed on Him.

My legs felt like lead as I trudged up the stairs to the finance office. Choking down self-pity, I tried to recenter my thoughts. I wanted to believe *His* plan remained intact. But, in that moment, it was a hard plan to reconcile.

Silently, I begged God to make me brave. (Translation: I was dangerously close to a full-blown meltdown). Despite the lump in my throat and the knot in my gut, I wanted to express my gratitude to the staff. My professors had poured into every facet of my life—welcoming me into their homes and helping me wrestle through hard theological questions. Their investment shaped me into a stronger woman of faith. I would always hold them in the highest esteem.

The school president, bursar, and a third, less-impressive individual in bib overalls greeted me. He looked like the farmer I had seen that morning, lumbering up the hill in an old pickup with a load of apples. I had even waved to him, thrilled to add something other than plums to our usual fruit option.

Without small talk, the president introduced me to the farmer—his friend, Don. *"Uh...hi. Nice to meet you."* As the words came out, I knew they weren't true. I didn't want to meet anyone, especially right now when I was about to confirm my hard decision in front of a stranger.

It turned out Don was, indeed, the apple farmer. He met with our president earlier that day, expressing a desire to assist a struggling student. In hindsight, I suppose my weekly trip to the finance office served as God's way of bringing a particular *'struggling student'* to mind.

I was chosen as the recipient of Don's generosity. I couldn't stop the tears, nor did I try. They spilled silently onto my lap, a speechless offering of gratitude.

I was awestruck. God had provided yet another step forward in my education. The three witnesses simply smiled. It was a sacred moment—marked with laughter and tears.

The apple farmer leaned forward. His gaze overflowed with compassion. What he said next exceeded my wildest imagination: *"Patty, it's so good to meet you. This morning, I had the privilege of seeing your grades and hearing about your weekly trips to this office. I want to encourage you to keep up the hard work. I am going to contact this office every semester—**until you graduate**—and I will cover any outstanding balance on your account. You are not to worry another day about finishing your education."*

In that moment, I recognized how vastly I had underestimated God's generosity.

Over the next three years, I was freed from the burden of financial worry. This dear apple farmer watched over my account like a hen brooding over her chicks, until the day I earned my degree. Not long after that, he went home to be with the Lord.

This story still takes my breath away. It brings me to my knees when I consider the love of a Father who longs to *accomplish immeasurably more than all we ask or imagine. (Ephesians 3:20-21 NLT).*

God prompted an old apple farmer to deliver a load of apples to a private college—on the very day my future hung in the balance. The farmer listened. And God met a nineteen-year-old girl who came to Him with empty hands and a desperate prayer.

After losing Karissa, that memory of God's involvement mattered. I had been out of options then—and I was out of options now. Only this time, it wasn't my bank account that was depleted. It was my soul.

I reached back, recalling the ways God had worked beyond my imagination—silently, personally, unmistakably. Long before I had language for it, He had been revealing Himself as **My Place of Provision**. Long before I knew how desperately I would need to hide in Him, He was revealing His generous, creative heart:

"*Open wide your mouth and I will fill it.*
I will give you wild honey from a rock."
Psalm 81:10b,16 (NIV)

As I sat with those words, I knew the only One capable of filling my empty hands and aching arms was the God who refused to be confined to predictable solutions— the God who satisfies His children through means we would never imagine.

Wild honey from a rock.

Since bees don't produce honey in stone, I began to wonder if God was inviting me—not to understand His provision—but to trust Him for it, even when it arrived in forms I wouldn't know to ask for.

In the empty days of grief, I didn't always remember to run to Him. Hardship had a way of clouding my view of His tender care. It was easy to lose confidence and collapse under the crush of doubt.

Instead of casting my cares on God, I was often bent beneath the weight of them.

One of my favorite poems confesses this very struggle:

"It is His will that I should cast
My care on Him each day.
He also bids me not to cast
My confidence away.
But Oh! How foolishly I act,
When taken unaware.
I cast away my confidence,
And carry all my care."[xix]

This has been so true of me. Yet, God continues to beckon:

Give your burdens to Me and I will sustain you.
(Psalm 55:22 paraphrased)

I came to realize that He is not appalled by our emptiness or overwhelmed by our need.

His help is unbridled. His resources unlimited. His joy is complete when we enter His presence, opening our empty hands to the only One who can fill us.

Sometimes provision may accompany a load of apples. Sometimes it might look like just enough courage for the next step. And sometimes, it simply looks like being held when empty hands are all we have to offer.

CHAPTER 11

PROVISION IN DISGUISE

God can do anything, you know—far more than you could ever
imagine or guess or request in your wildest dreams!
Ephesians 3:20 (MSG)

The Bug in God's Battle Plan

Doubt knew how to find the fine crack in my soul and slip in, causing me to second-guess God's goodness. Maybe you've carried some of those same doubts, believing God answers prayer, but—your prayers? Your crushing needs? If you have questioned God's desire to respond to your manifold burdens, you're not alone.

Doubt clung to my soul like gum to a shoe—I'm pretty sure it's been that way for us since Eden. A gnawing urge to question life—and God—is woven into our very fabric. By the time we blow out the second candle on our birthday cake, we've already mastered the art of questioning.

"*Why?*"

This one-syllable word embodies a thousand feelings—curiosity, hope, anger, confusion, and longing. Some questions draw us closer to God; others drive us from Him in defiant pain.

After losing Karissa, *"why"* became the language of my prayers. I sounded like a broken record, whispering it in grief. I shouted it in frustration. And sometimes, it still slips out in the most ordinary moments.

The table was set. Soft music filled the air. Candlelight warmed the patio as ribs sizzled on the grill—everything poised for an unhurried night with dear friends. But as Gary pulled the ribs off the grill, the evening unraveled. Hornets swarmed the platter, like Nazi warplanes descending in WWII. A few brave souls swatted in vain while the rest of us ran inside like track stars at the sound of the starting gun. Let's just say—the memories we made that night were not the ones I'd planned.

That swarm stirred more than our guests—it stirred a question I took straight to God. *"Seriously, Lord... why the hornets?"*

From my vantage point, they serve no redeeming purpose. They don't make honey. They don't seem to control pests. Hornets are the bullies at the barbecue—disruptors of peace, champions of chaos and pain.

Though I didn't expect a response, a few days later I stumbled on an account in Scripture that stopped me in my tracks. God's people were cornered by the Amorites—outnumbered, outmatched, and facing what looked like certain defeat. Their soldiers closed in on Israel's camp like a vice-grip, ready to crush them.

I imagined how terrified the Israelites must have felt that day: No "*good mornings.*" No chatter. Just the silence of dread. And then God did something astonishing:

"I sent the hornets ahead of you,
which drove them out before you—also the two Amorite kings.
You did not do it with your own sword and bow."
Joshua 24:12 (NIV)

Hornets. Not strategy. Not strength. Not a battle plan anyone would have drafted.

Just hornets.

That verse stayed with me—not because I suddenly appreciated them—but because it disrupted my assumptions of how God works. He has never been limited to human strategies. He would never be confined to what makes sense. He can use anything in His creation to accomplish His purpose—even those pesky creatures I'd written off as unnecessary and cruel.

And somehow—in the chaos of pain, that mattered to me.

A Box Full of Kittens

Weeks had slipped by since the marriage retreat. My conference declaration was as brittle as the cracked sculpture I'd formed. That tender prayer had slowly turned sharper, and more impatient:

"My arms still hang limp—God, why won't You lift them? My hands remain empty, waiting for You to fill them."

I once read, *"You never get over loss. You just learn to live with it."*[xx] Honestly, that felt unbearably bleak. How was I supposed to *live* with this vast emptiness? The void was heavy—suffocating.

Then the doorbell rang, yanking me from this moment of silent ache.

I opened the door. No one was there. Then I looked down—and locked eyes with a scrawny cat in a cardboard box, surrounded by a litter of wide-eyed kittens.

Seriously, God?

For context: I'm a dog person--any size, almost any breed. But cats? No offense—it's a hard pass. As a baby, I nearly suffocated when our family cat curled up on my face after a warm bottle. I was found blue-faced. That cat was re-homed the same day, and cats were permanently canceled.

Besides, my husband is deathly allergic to cats. This was one of the few areas where we would always be in full agreement.

Until now.

Here they were—meowing, helpless, abandoned, and needing a family as desperately as I needed someone—something—to care for. And to my surprise, compassion stirred. Using a litter of kittens as a healing balm for my heart felt as absurd as sending hornets to win a war.

Yet, as I reached into the box, my heart softened. These playful kittens filled my empty hands with warmth. Soft purrs broke the silence. My heart, long weighted down, lifted—long enough to breathe.

Mama cat, true to my suspicions, wanted nothing to do with me. I became her full-time nanny while she disappeared into a nearby field for hours. Then one day she vanished for good.

I began to notice something:

Right in the middle of my waiting, my accusing, my doubt —God met me in a way I would have never requested. Kittens—small, living creatures, became reminders on an unwanted path: I was still seen.

Maybe you carry the same doubt: *Does God see my emptiness? The ache in my soul?*

I'm convinced, if God could send an apple-farmer to fund a student's needs, hornets to defeat an army, or kittens to fill lifeless arms—He can employ anything in creation to satisfy the need in *your* soul.

Nothing is off-limits for the God who provides.

El Shaddai

Nursing Karissa had been one of the most sacred rhythms of motherhood. Life slowed. A deep bond formed between us as her small body molded to mine. It was a picture of peace and contentment. I marveled that my body could supply everything she needed for growth. Her sighs, her relaxed limbs, spoke of one thing: satisfaction.

Now, I felt like an infant myself—longing to be held and filled with that kind of soul-deep nourishment. Without it, I felt like an abandoned child, afraid that true contentment and steady growth might remain forever out of reach. I sensed that God's Word could quiet the ache in my soul… but on this hard path, the Bible felt too heavy to pick up.

As memories of God's former provision kept surfacing, gratitude grew—but so did a quieter question beneath it: *Would He ever satisfy this deep ache?*

Around that time, I began reading a book about the names of God. One name stopped me: *El Shaddai—"The Lord Almighty"*. It carried the immovable strength of a mountain, yet also the tender sufficiency of a mother's care. Strength and nurture held together in one name.[xxi]

Its Hebrew root *shad* (שַׁד), means "breast."[xxii] That shocked me. But the meaning was unmistakably intimate: God was being revealed as One who nourishes, supplies, and sustains—He's strong but also near. Personal. Attentive. It was the kind of care my soul was craving.

Scripture began to sound different in that light:

Like newborn babies, long for the pure milk of the word,
so that by it you may grow in respect to salvation.
1 Peter 2:2 (NASB)

I noticed ways doubt had quietly distanced me from *El Shaddai*. That distance left me dry and disillusioned. The world offered plenty of substitutes—distractions, comforts, noise—but none of them touched the ache or quenched the thirst beneath it.

I wondered if this emptiness was part of grief itself. Did loss always stir this ache to be held, to be nourished in ways we can't name? Those questions rose like a tide, and I let them.

Then, one afternoon, alone in my living room, I cried out to God from the cavern of my pain. I didn't ask for answers. I asked to be fed. I held my Bible in my lap. I didn't want to skim or search for something quick. I simply wanted to receive anything He desired to provide. I told God the truth:

"I'm starving. I'm weary. God, I need You. Would you feed me?"

Then, slowly… I opened it, picturing myself climbing into El Shaddai's arms. I rested my head against His chest and listened to His heart. I invited Him to fill the hollow places with the nourishment only He could give.

He was becoming *My Place of Provision*—showing me how He could satisfy the hunger nothing else had been able to reach.

The Gift of Emptiness

Yet, God's provision didn't always feel abundant. There were days when I simply wondered, "*How long, Lord?*"

I read about Israel—freed from slavery through a cascade of miracles—and I'm struck by how quickly celebration gave way to complaint. The desert was dry. Barren. A place of lack. And when their stomachs rumbled, so did their questions: *Where is the food? Did you bring us out here to die?* (See Exodus 1–16)

I used to read those passages with a sense of annoyance—until I recognized myself among the grumblers.

When life felt threatening, I craved more than what God seemed to be offering. I questioned His provision and forgot His faithfulness. And yet—because of His mercy—I can trace the ways He fed me anyway. Just as He did for them.

God answered their complaints, not with rebuke but with manna—daily bread from heaven. It fell like dew, tasting as sweet as honey wafers. I tried to imagine it: a bone-weary, wandering people waking up morning after morning—thousands of mornings—to a landscape dusted with divine provision. Not excess. Not a month's worth of food. Just enough. Bite-sized portions of daily grace.

Though the Israelites wandered for forty years, God never withdrew His care. I was learning to see that same patience at work in my own story. Even when I felt undeserving, He continued to nourish me.

When Jesus later told the crowd, *"I am the bread of life. Whoever comes to Me will never go hungry, and whoever believes in Me will never be thirsty," (See John 6:35)* His words no longer sounded abstract. They sounded personal—like an invitation spoken to all of us who feel empty.

As I retrace my story, I wonder where you might find yourself today. Maybe you're carrying a quiet, persistent hunger of your own. I don't have a formula to offer you. I only know this: He never turned me away. El Shaddai—*The Place of Provision*—met me with strength and nourishment even when I had nothing left to keep going.

There were moments I was afraid to move on—afraid healing would mean forgetting Karissa. I was afraid to believe anything good could grow from what felt so barren. And still, God kept asking a question that lingered in my heart:

"Is anything too hard for the Lord?"
Genesis 18:14 (NIV)

I didn't answer that question—but I tried hard to listen.

Over time, I was able to receive nourishment from Scripture. I saw that my emptiness wasn't failure. It was a place of invitation—a place of encounter. *The Place* where provision arrived daily, faithfully, and freely.

"Come... let the one who is thirsty come;
and let the one who wishes take the free gift of the water of life."
Revelation 22:17b (NIV)

This is where I found myself—returning to Him day after day—lifting empty hands to the One ready to give—grace in portions I could carry.

And in that place of need, I discovered what I never would have chosen: emptiness became the doorway through which provision entered.

"God can do anything, you know—far more than
you could ever
imagine or guess or request in your wildest
dreams."
Ephesians 3:20 (MSG)

CHAPTER 12

A LITTLE HELP FROM MY FRIENDS

Two are better than one... a cord of three strands is not quickly broken.
Ecclesiastes 4:9a, 12b (CSB)

For this brief season, my box of beloved kittens was hidden manna—tangible comfort in my grief. But God also sent another kind of manna: a compassionate band of sisters who set aside their own needs to tend to my shattered heart. They organized a schedule so I was rarely alone for too long. They showed up, day after day—an unwavering presence for their emotionally broken friend.

They didn't try to fix me or rush me forward. They didn't force words into the silence. They simply stayed near, reminding me I wasn't alone.

As they sat at my table—reading, balancing checkbooks, updating calendars, writing letters—I slowly found the courage to re-enter life's simplest tasks. Their companionship quieted the accusations and dark imaginations that haunted my mind. When I had no strength to fight for myself, they fought for me.

I'm convinced my soul would have collapsed beneath the weight of grief if I had carried it alone. But these women shouldered the load with me—sometimes without saying a word. They wept with me. Held me when I couldn't stand. With careful restraint, they reminded me of God's love without pressing truths I still struggled to embrace.

We spoke honestly with one another. They admitted their fear of saying Karissa's name, worried it would deepen my pain. I told them I needed to hear it—to know others remembered her. Their willingness to risk getting it wrong, to show up with their own uncertainty, forged a friendship marked by trust and tenderness.

Grief is grimy work. I will always be grateful for friends who knelt beside me in the mud without waiting to feel prepared. They didn't need degrees in grief counseling—just the courage to step into the mess. Looking back, I wonder if I would have recognized God's daily provision at all, had He not shown up at my door with skin on.

Birthday Wishes

Wanda was one of the friends who stood beside me—steadfast in my grief. She carried my longing for another child to the Lord—without questioning the timing or diminishing my hope. She prayed faithfully for Gary and me, asking God to give us another child. We had shared our first pregnancies together—her son was born just weeks after Karissa. We dreamed of doing it all again, side by side, raising our kids together.

As my twenty-fourth birthday neared, I couldn't ignore the possibility—my cycle was several days late. Ironically, Wanda's was too. We decided my birthday would be the perfect day to confirm our hopes. That morning, we arrived at the lab early enough to ensure same-day results. By afternoon, we'd be heading to the mountains with our husbands and two other couples. Whether we skied or stayed inside depended on what the results revealed.

The day crawled. My heart pounded every time the phone rang. Would this be my birthday gift from heaven?

Minutes before leaving, we got our results. Wanda was pregnant—I was not.

Shame crept in as jealousy whispered, *"God it's my birthday. Where is my blessing?"* While my arms remained empty, God blessed my friend with another child. I wanted to celebrate Wanda's news—she was gracious and deeply deserving—but today? On my birthday? I felt abandoned. Forgotten.

The couples had planned to drive separately—I was grateful for that decision. The two-hour drive gave me space to unravel. I didn't want to talk—not to Gary, not to anyone. Tears threatened with every breath. I reached for my Bible, desperate for something—anything that might explain God's silence.

Before opening it, I whispered the only honest prayer I had left.

"God, I feel so let down. All I wanted was the one gift only You could give—but You withheld it, and I don't understand why."

That was it. No polish. Just emptiness.

I opened my Bible and landed in Leviticus—hardly the place you turn when drowning in disappointment. Laws. Regulations. Rituals. Not exactly intended to soothe or comfort a grieving soul. But God delights in meeting us in unlikely places. Apparently, this included Leviticus.

Before despair could pull me under, an ancient promise rose from the page and met me in my ache—so intimate it stole my breath:

> *"'I will look on you with favor and will make you fruitful and will increase your numbers. I will keep my covenant with you. You will still be eating last year's harvest when you will have to move it out to make room for the new. I will put my dwelling place among you, and I will not abhor you. I will walk among you and be your God, and you will be my people. I am the Lord*

your God... I broke the bars of your yoke and enabled you to walk with heads held high.
Leviticus 26:9-11(NIV)

These words, once spoken to a people emerging from bondage, breathed hope into me. They were God's manna for my sorrow: the sustenance I needed to trust His heart, even when I couldn't trace His hand.

I hadn't received what I longed for—but I knew God was present—even here in the waiting. Clutching my Bible to my chest, I sensed that my deepest longings were safe with Him.

Two hours later, we arrived at the cabin. I was no longer drowning in a swamp of self-pity. Did I have all the answers? No. Did I understand why things had unfolded this way? Not at all. But God's unfailing love had steadied me, and for the moment, it was enough.

Pastor and author Mark Batterson captures it well: "*Faith is not logical. But it isn't illogical either. Faith is theological. It does not ignore reality; it just adds God into the equation.*"[xxiii]

I offered my empty womb as a sacred space—unsure of what provision would look like but trusting He would meet me there. My longings had not led me to despair—they had led me to Him. To the Place of Provision. To El Shaddai—The All-Sufficient One.

LORD, you know the hopes of the helpless.
Surely you will hear their cries and comfort them.
Psalm 10:17 (NLT)

You've Got Mail

Days blurred together, weaving weeks into an unrelenting march. The world moved forward, largely unaware of those lagging behind. Medical bills landed like boulders—each one a fresh reminder of how powerless man is to stop death. The wounds reopened with every unsealed envelope. How cruel, how ironic, to be charged for an ambulance that carried your daughter away from your life.

As months passed, visits from friends grew less frequent. Sympathy cards thinned. Life, for everyone else, resumed its usual rhythm.

I envied my friends' ability to step back into normalcy, while my own existence felt permanently out of sync.

Before long, my growing kittens—a balm in my suffering—would need homes beyond our shed. I wondered what would replace their sweet comfort when they were gone? I didn't know the answer. I only knew I felt the ache of what was slipping away.

On one of those raw afternoons, I shuffled to the mailbox at the end of the driveway. A few bills. A trickle of sympathy cards. And one thin envelope—lightweight, with no return address. I tossed the bills on the kitchen counter. They could wait.

I sank onto the couch with the cards. Each one reminded me that someone who still remembered. They had paused their life long enough to reach toward us—to ease our pain. They were companions on our journey-- hands holding mine when my strength gave out.

Finally, I opened the thin envelope. Inside was a hand-cut paper heart with a hand-written verse—with my name on it:

Patty, "Can a mother forget the baby at her breast
and have not compassion on the child she has born?
Though she could forget, I cannot forget you. See, I have
Engraved your name on the palms of my hands.
Your walls are ever before me."
Isaiah 49:15-16 NIV

Too weary to search the Scripture on my own, the Living Word found me. The question arrested my grief-fogged mind: *Can a mother forget the baby in her arms?*

The answer rose instantly—I wanted to scream it.

No. Never.

Even if she could possibly forget... I cannot forget you.

In that moment, a lie I had been quietly carrying was exposed—that I had somehow been overlooked, punished, set aside.

The verse didn't erase my questions or immediately mend my heart, but it steadied me. It whispered what I needed to hear: *I have not forgotten you. I cannot forget you. It is impossible, Patty. I've engraved a tattoo on My hand, and your name is on it.*

I wasn't asked to understand the timing or the pain—only to trust that God was still with me in it. He could no more forget me than I could forget Karissa. God still held me close to His heart.

The mailman continued delivering these handwritten verses. I tucked each one into my Bible, savored it like bread for a starving soul. Something in me began to change. I wasn't immediately healed. I wasn't 'better'. But I didn't feel alone in my questions.

I was recognizing God's Voice through His Word again. It began dismantling the distorted thoughts that grief had wallpapered over my mind, replacing them with truth I could return to when the days grew heavy.

Trust didn't come easily. It took months—long months—to relearn that I was still His beloved child even when circumstances were brutal. Even when nothing made sense.

Your situation—and mine—are always before Him. Your name, like mine, is engraved on His hands. His door is always open to us. And when we come with empty hands and unanswered questions, we are met not with impatience—but with grace and mercy, right in the middle of our need.

INVITING GOD TO BECOME YOUR PLACE OF PROVISION

One of the things I treasure most about God's Word is how it reveals His heart toward us. Scripture is more than a collection of stories—it is God's own book, unveiling both His majestic power and His intimate care. We can miss God's deepest message if we only look for ourselves within its pages. But when we seek Him—His fingerprints, His character, His voice—we discover, not just His power, but His tender care for ordinary people like you and me.

He knows exactly what His children need. And in both miraculous and quiet ways, He meets us—sometimes in ways we don't expect, and often much more slowly than we'd choose.

God invites our suffering hearts into His redemptive story, weaving our longings, losses, and lives into something held by His care.

An Anchor of Help in a World of Hurt

When you feel ready, return to some of the passages you encountered in this section. **You may want to read just one—or sit with a single line that feels meaningful to you.**

- *Ephesians 3:20*
- *Psalm 81:10b*
- *Leviticus 26:9-11*

After you've pondered a verse or a line, close your eyes and just breathe—slowly.

Ask: ***God, is there anything You want me to notice right now?*** There is no pressure to hear something. You may have caught a faint impression or even a phrase that became a source of encouragement.

Write down anything you want to remember. Is there anything you noticed about God's nature that you didn't recognize before?

Provision Remembered

Reflect on a time—recent or long ago—when God met you in an unexpected way. It may have come through a person, a verse, a circumstance, or through something you hadn't recognized as provision until much later. What came to mind? How did it shift your perspective or renew your hope?

Provision Needed

Now consider where you feel most empty or stretched thin today? Take a moment to name those places before Him. Don't rush. Invite Him into that space.

Ask: *Lord, would You meet me here? Would You be my Place of Provision today—in whatever way You choose?*

Write: If you'd like, write a simple prayer—perhaps a few words of gratitude (for what He's done) and a prayer of trust (for what you're still bringing to Him).

A Prayer when You Feel Empty

Oh, Place of Provision,
I come to You—my loving and compassionate Father.
You take in hand the trouble of the afflicted.
You know the hopes of the helpless.
You hear my cries and comfort me.
I run to you with unquenchable thirst,
these empty hands…and cavernous longings.
(Psalm 10:14,17 - Paraphrased)

You alone can fill what is hollow in me.
You alone are enough.
I yield my life to your goodness.
As you supplied manna to Your people in the wilderness,
would You meet me in this barren place?
I don't even know what my soul needs most, but You do.
You ride across the heavens to help me. (Deuteronomy 33:26)
You are my God, My Place of Provision.
So, I run to You—
and trust You to be enough.
Amen.

SECTION FIVE

The Place of Protection

For All My Fear

The Lord rescues the godly;
he is their fortress in times of trouble.

Psalm 37:39 NLT

CHAPTER 13

TEARS AND TIDES

Be my mighty rock,
the place where I can always run for protection.
Psalm 71:3 (CEV)

Karissa's death shattered my theology on suffering. It breached what I believed were impenetrable walls surrounding God's children. Suddenly I felt exposed, like someone crouching behind fractured walls, unsure what might come next.

What other evils loomed on our horizon?

Fear became paralyzing. Would Gary be taken from me next? Would another tragedy ambush our lives? Later, I came to understand how common those fears are after great loss. When security is violently shaken, the soul lives on high alert—bracing for the next blow. Remaining in that state for long is exhausting. It drains something deep.

Perhaps you understand.

During my darkest days, when fear pressed in from every direction, a realization began to surface: God understood my vulnerability. He knows how easily fear takes ground in the human heart. Perhaps that is why Scripture so often whispers, *"Do not fear."* It appears 365 times—one for every day of the year.[xxiv]

The assurance dawned slowly. I didn't have to surrender my life to fear.

Familiar stories from Scripture steadied me. One rose again and again—Moses leading the Israelites out of slavery. But freedom didn't remove danger. They found themselves trapped—an army behind them, the Red Sea before them.

Scripture records it plainly: "*They were terrified and cried out to the Lord.*" Exodus 14:10 (NIV)

I can almost hear it—two million anguished voices!

Then, cutting through the chaos, Moses spoke: *"Do not be afraid. Stand firm and you will see the deliverance the Lord will bring you today... The Lord will fight for you; you need only to* ***be still****."* Exodus 14:13-14 (NIV)

Be still?

That felt impossible.

In the years since losing Karissa, I have learned that trusting God in crisis is one of the most difficult disciplines of faith. Yet it was my only way forward. The only way out of fear was to stand still long enough to believe that the God who began this deliverance would complete it.

When I felt pinned between grief and the unknown, I called out to Him. And often, in that suffocating in-between, I could sense God's response, *"Be still. Watch what I will do. I will fight for you."*

Even now, I must remind myself daily to invite Him into what unsettles me. Because without Him, I will never be still.

A Surprise Vacation

In those early weeks after Karissa's death, even simple tasks felt mentally exhausting. Every action reminded me of her absence. Running bathwater made me ache for the simple joy of bathing her. Folding laundry awakened the longing to hold her tiny clothes. Preparing dinner stirred memories of steaming and blending her sweet potatoes and carrots.

Grief rewrote everything.

I remain deeply grateful for our church family during those painful days. They were alert to our unspoken needs and stepped in to lighten our load. About a month after Karissa's memorial, our pastor handed us a card.

Inside was something we could never imagine: an all-expenses-paid trip to Hawaii.

To this day, we don't know the individuals involved in arranging it. Their gift was meant to offer us rest—a way to lift us from our sorrow-soaked surroundings, into a space where beauty might begin to overshadow grief. Our friends hoped this trip might afford us an opportunity to create new memories and provide a brief reprieve from the gnawing ache of our current circumstances.

Tropical air and warm island greetings welcomed us to paradise. Orchid leis were slipped over our shoulders. Turquoise water shimmered in the sun. I tried to quiet the mental whisper: *"Karissa would have loved this."*

But paradise does not erase loss. The same broken couple who boarded the plane in Los Angeles arrived in Hawaii. Wherever you go, there you are.

Families were everywhere—strollers, toddlers on shoulders, babies' content in their mothers' arms. The sight of these happy families wrenched like a knife. My arms ached.

To escape the crowds, Gary and I rented mopeds and ventured beyond the city. We laughed through dinners well beyond our budget—fumbling with too many forks and unfamiliar etiquette. We were out of our league, and for those few moments, we enjoyed it.

One evening, after dinner, we walked along the beach. The warm sand soothed our feet. My lei perfumed the night air. The moon shimmered across a calm sea.

For the first time in weeks, I noticed beauty all around me.

We sat together in the sand, listening to the slow rhythm of the waves. In the quiet, our thoughts drifted back to a recent memory: Karissa's first—and only—trip to the movies. How fitting that it had been *An American Tail*, a Disney film about a brave little mouse separated from his family.

Lost in a vast and lonely world, both he and his parents clung to the same fragile hope—that love would somehow guide them back to one another.

In the end, it did.

Oh, to live in a world where stories always end that way—where those dreams come true. I didn't try to hold back tears. In the real world, our dreams do not always come true.

Beauty was everywhere… but so was grief.

I slipped the damp lei from my neck—its petals heavy with my steady stream of pain. Walking toward the water's edge, I gently released it into the tide.

"Oh God," I prayed, *"would You let Karissa know we are thinking about her—loving her tonight? Let her see this small floating gift from her mommy."*

We stood there until all our tears and our aching prayers were carried away into the moonlit ocean. Finally, we walked hand in hand back to our mopeds, hearts still broken. But something in my soul had softened.

Not healed. Not whole.

Just softened enough to sense it again—the quiet kindness of God. The comfort of our memories. The mystery of a love even death could not silence.

CHAPTER 14

A FORTRESS IN THE NIGHT

In my distress I called to the LORD;
I cried to my God for help.
From his temple he heard my voice;
my cry came before him, into his ears.
Psalm 18:6 (NIV)

It had been a full and lovely day. The anonymity of this Hawaiian paradise brought unexpected relief—our wound felt hidden on the island, less exposed to the watching world. For a moment, we could breathe again.

Looking back, I now realize how differently Gary and I were processing our pain. He returned to work immediately after Karissa's memorial, pouring himself into our growing youth ministry. It offered a daily distraction from grief.

His friends, unsure how to support him emotionally, defaulted to activities designed to distract—pickup basketball games, racquetball matches—anything to keep things light. While I felt paralyzed in sorrow, Gary appeared strong and steady, pressing forward, serving others, and—at least on the surface—enjoying life. I lagged behind, riding one emotional rollercoaster after another.

Exhausted from a long day of travel and island adventures, we collapsed into bed. In the early days after Karissa's death, intimacy had taken on a different form. Comfort was found in simply holding one other—a quiet reassurance we were not alone in this living hell. That night, sleep came quickly.

But, sometime in the middle of the night, distressing moans broke through the stillness. They swelled into blood-curdling screams. At first, I thought something terrible was happening just outside our room. But as I sat up, I realized the horror was beside me. Gary was thrashing, gripped by unimaginable terror. I struggled to wake him.

When I finally did, he described his nightmare—vivid, awful images surrounding Karissa's final moments. Hearing it spoken aloud was both painful and haunting. I hoped that giving voice to it might loosen the grip of the trauma Gary had experienced in discovering Karissa's lifeless body.

But as with many dreams, this one reshaped reality into something distorted and terrifying.: "*I was reaching for Karissa. She was in the arms of what I thought was an angelic being sent to help her—until the figure turned, and I realized it was an evil presence, stealing her from me.*"

Listening to his torment deepened my own fear and vulnerability.

The nightmares didn't end that night. They became a recurring torment—always the same dream.

Instead of ending the full vacation days with sweet intimacy, I began to dread bedtime. We would collapse into bed, only to be jolted awake hours later by Gary's screams—night after night. In desperation, I'd try to shake him into awareness—to bring him back to reality. The weight of it all grew unbearable.

One night, midway through our vacation, I hit my breaking point and whispered words that stabbed even as I spoke them: *Gary, I've been hanging on by a thread these past few weeks. It's not getting better. In fact, the pain feels worse. I don't know if I can do this anymore. Maybe this would all stop if we went our separate ways—left the past behind, and trusted God for a fresh start. This journey... it's just too painful to bear together.*

(I don't think this was what our friends had in mind when they arranged this tropical get-away.)

As those death-laced words left my lips, Gary's eyes filled with tears—not from anger or judgment. He understood many couples didn't survive this level of trauma. The illusion that escape is possible—the hope that *a fresh start* might stop the internal bleeding—has unraveled many relationships.

While my emotions were volatile, Gary's remained steady. I had mistaken his steadiness as being detached from our loss, yet he had somehow found a quiet assurance: God would hold us together.

His words came slowly, with no desire to argue or persuade, but to lift me above the chaos: *"Patty, as hard as this is to walk through the uncertainty of our grief, do you really think it will become easier to carry this sorrow alone? I don't want to bear it without you. No one else will understand your deep love for Karissa or comprehend what it meant to be her parents. That love has the power to fasten our hearts to one another."*

Gary's gentle words steadied me in the wreckage of my regretted ones. God used him to expose the enemy's fear tactics—attempting to divide what grief had already weakened. In the tenderness of that raw moment, it felt as though God breathed on the faint embers of trust, barely aglow in my soul. It was as if the Word—stored deep within me—finally found enough air to flicker.

BE STILL.

Slowly those words became less of a command and more of an invitation. They began to rise within me, casting a soft light on the lies my terrified mind had entertained. They illuminated what I had nearly forgotten: we were not beyond God's reach. He would not leave us alone.

Was it possible this pain would not be the end of our story?

There—on that bed—I turned toward Gary's open arms and let him hold me. And there—where sorrow had built its wall between us—a door of mercy quietly opened. What I thought was the end began to feel like the smallest beginning.

Years later, David's psalm would give language to what we experienced that night:

Those who go to God Most High for safety
will be protected by the Almighty.
I will say to the LORD,
*"You are **My Place** of safety and protection.*
You are my God and I trust you."
Psalm 91:1-2 (NCV - The Everyday Bible)

God welcomed our trembling hearts into His *Place of Protection*, sheltering us from the terrors that threatened not only to devour our individual lives, but to unravel the bond between us. His protection steadied us.

This was not my journey to walk alone. It was not Gary's either. This was *our* story—one we would somehow carry together. Our resolve was not bold or heroic. We knew the road ahead might be steeper than we felt prepared for—but within the shelter of the Most-High, we would not walk it unchanged.

That night, before surrendering to our desperate need for rest, we placed our hands on one another's heads and asked God to guard every hidden, restless thought. When morning light slipped through the curtains, we realized we had slept for hours. Our bodies had rested. God had answered.

This battle did not disappear. It continued—most fiercely in the quiet theater of our minds. Fear thrives there, twisting truth in the dark with cords of doubt and deception.

But we remembered God's promise: He doesn't leave us unprotected. One of His generous gifts—often overlooked until crisis reveals its necessity—is the armor God provides. (See Ephesians 6:10-18). The helmet of salvation mattered deeply in that season. Placed over our minds, it reminded us that God guards everything we entrust to Him.

So, night after night, we returned to the same simple practice—praying over one another's thoughts, surrendering what we could not control into God's care. Gradually, terror loosened its grip. And then, one day, the nightmares stopped.

We found rest—not because the battle vanished, but because God stood watch. Again and again, we ran to Him with our fears and discovered what He had promised all along: We were safe in His everlasting arms.

Grief did not become easier—only different. I wanted to talk about Karissa constantly—with everyone. Gary felt more guarded, sensing the teenage girl scooping our ice cream might not know what to do with the sacred complexity of our pain. But as we learned to honor those differences instead of resenting them, we began to see how each response carried its own strength. Slowly, the weight grief placed on our marriage began to lift.

I would learn—slowly—to believe victory over fear is not loud or dramatic. It grows quietly in those who remain in *The Place of*

Protection. And perhaps this requires something far simpler than strength.

Come—As a Child

As a child I wrestled with many fears— some born from frightening dreams and imagined monsters lurking in the dark. I wore a path between my bedroom and my parents' room, knowing exactly where to run for refuge. My mom would wrap her arms around me and whisper reassurance until fear lost its grip.

In a healthy home, a child instinctively knows where to run. And within that embrace comes wave after wave of assurance: *Nothing can touch me now.*

This is a tender reflection of the security we find in the Father's love. His presence stills our fears and wraps us in unshakable safety.

Jesus came to reveal the Father's heart. (See John 1:18 and John 14:9) We see His heart clearly in the way He welcomed children. He didn't ask them to wait their turn or keep a respectful distance. In a culture that placed little value on children, He drew them near.

The disciples struggled to understand. To them, protecting the "real" ministry—like healing the sick, helping the lame walk, restoring sight to the blind—required His full attention. But what if these noisy, carefree children were not interruptions at all? What if they were the model of life in His kingdom?

Jesus became indignant with his disciples and said,

"Let the little children come to me.
Don't stop them,
because the kingdom of God
belongs to those who are like these children."
Mark 10:14 (NLT)

Because the disciples could not yet grasp what God's kingdom looked like, Jesus showed them: it belongs to those who come like children—unhindered, unashamed, and confident in His care.

In the midst of my grief, I longed for that childlike heart again, to run to *The Place of Protection,* fully confident in his care.

Regardless of our age, background, or position, His invitation remains:

"Come. Run to me with your fears, your joys, and the questions too heavy to carry alone. You are not an interruption. You're not a burden or a distraction. Nothing on my agenda is more important than this moment—with you."

One day my heart would resonate deeply with the psalmist:

My heart has heard you say, "Come and talk with me."
And my heart responds, "Lord, I am coming."
Psalm 27:8 (NLT)

It seems everyone—from leper to legislator, pauper to prince, child to king—is invited.

Perhaps responding to His invitation is the greatest gift we can offer our souls.

So why not close this book for a moment and answer Him?

"Lord, I am coming."

Run to Him with your questions, your shattered heart, and your clenched fists. He is *The Place* where fear dissolves within the shelter of His protection.

CHAPTER 15

NEVER ALONE

But you, O LORD, are a shield about me,
my glory, and the lifter of my head.
I cried aloud to the LORD,
and he answered me from his holy hill. Selah
I lay down and slept;
I woke again, for the LORD sustained me.
Psalm 3:3-6 (ESV)

We found incredible safety in God's arms—but grief doesn't vanish overnight. As you have probably discovered, healing is rarely linear. Moments of peace and clarity are often hijacked by waves of sorrow that crash down without warning.

While alert to the uncertainty within a new day, we were determined to move forward, carrying both the pain and the awe of this vacation into whatever came next. We wanted to soak in every drop of joy this gift had to offer.

Busted Plates and Broken Hearts

An excursion to the Polynesian Cultural Center was the highlight of the day's itinerary. We spent hours under the Hawaiian sun, immersed in the customs and traditions of the Pacific Islands. We threw ourselves into hands-on activities—trying our best (and failing gloriously) at games of skill, canoe paddling, fire-starting, cooking, and even hula dancing. *How long had it been since we laughed this hard?*

For a few precious hours, joy broke through the heaviness. We remembered what it felt like to be lighthearted. To smile without effort.

The day ended with a grand, buffet-style luau. As we waited in line, the aroma of roasted meats and fresh pineapple drifted through the air, making our mouths water. A friendly man in front of Gary turned to strike up a conversation. As he shifted, his backpack swung unexpectedly, hitting Gary's plate with surprising precision. The plate slipped from his hands and crashed onto the concrete, shattering at his feet in a sharp spray of glass.

Embarrassed by the loud crash—after all, it was *his* plate—Gary sheepishly bent down to clean up the mess. Heads turned. The collective gasp came a split second later, as the reality of what had happened settled in. My knees buckled. My body swayed. A sharp shard had pierced a main artery in Gary's ankle. Within seconds, he was standing in a pool of blood.

Bystanders sprang into action. Someone called for an ambulance. Another knelt to compress the wound. With every beat of Gary's heart, more blood surged from his body. Paramedics arrived and raced us to a clinic in a remote village. He was quickly wheeled into a treatment room where the doctor calmly explained the procedure: "*He would need to probe the artery for fragments of glass. Each one had to be removed before the wound could be stitched and sealed.*"

As he spoke, I envisioned the procedure—and something inside me tilted. I've always hated the sight of blood—and this… was Gary's blood. The room began to spin.

They guided me to an empty lobby and asked me to wait—alone. What the nurse didn't realize was the enormity of her request. In the past five weeks, I could count on one hand the hours I had spent by myself. The last thing I wanted was to sit in an empty hospital waiting room, in a strange village, on an island far from home—with fear whispering in every shadow. But the nurse had more pressing concerns—Gary needed immediate attention.

I sank into the chair, panic rising. It hadn't even been six weeks since we were last ushered into a waiting room—one that had offered empty hope. That medical team couldn't save our baby girl. What if this one couldn't stop Gary's bleeding?

Time ticked on. Terror tightened its grip. *Why was it taking so long?*

I was no longer naïve to life's pain. I knew what it felt like to become part of a faceless statistic—just another number in a world where tragedy strikes, without discrimination. I used to believe God's protection meant He would never allow *that* to happen to me—whatever "that" unthinkable thing might be. But now, I lived in a world where the unimaginable could strike without warning, impaling hope in a single blow.

Would this doctor also step into the sterile waiting room with tears in his eyes, gently delivering those awful words I feared most? *"I'm so sorry. We tried everything..."* Were our last moments together in the cafeteria our final ones?

My mind spiraled—Where would I go tonight? Who would comfort me on this island? I imagined leaving this clinic alone, wandering into the dark, carrying an even heavier weight of razor-sharp grief. Each memory, another blade slicing through my already wounded heart. I wanted to flee this terrifying island and the pain it now carried.

From the ends of the earth,
I cry to you for help
when my heart is overwhelmed.
Lead me to the towering rock of safety,

for you are my safe refuge,
a fortress where my enemies cannot reach me.
*Psalm 61:2-3 (*NLT*)*

But somehow… into that suffocating space—between flickering hope and harsh fluorescent light, between worn vinyl chairs and a cold tile floor—the Spirit of God entered. Like a warrior appearing on the battlefield the moment before that fatal blow, He rushed in and sheltered me.

My Place—My Protection—entered that dismal waiting room long before I knew how the story would end. There, on a cracked vinyl chair, I felt hidden in His love and safe in His strength. His protection wasn't dependent on outcomes. It was rooted in His presence. Whatever the next moments held, He would guard my heart and mind. I closed my eyes, sensing His whisper: *I will never leave you nor forsake you. Joshua 1:5b (NIV)*

I am here.

My lungs expanded. My pulse slowed. This all-consuming love—too vast for my small understanding—covered me. Throughout my life, God had met me in unlikely places, just when I needed Him most. And here He was again, showing up in this forsaken waiting room, in a remote village, on this obscure night.

In the quiet, I felt as though He was inviting me to name what I needed most—not as a test of my faith, but as an act of trust in His care. To be honest, I wasn't sure I could name it. My need felt too vague to name. *I need You.* His Spirit began to remind me in the deepest place of my soul:

I am your peace. When fear threatened to overtake me, He was peace.

I am your comfort. In the room that felt too empty, He stayed.

I am your defender. When I felt exposed and powerless, He stood guard.

I am your protector. When my imagined future felt unbearable, He held me in the present moment.

I wasn't handed insights or promised outcomes. He offered me Himself.

Right there—in the middle of the unknown—He offered the fullness of who He is. Not later. Not once it was resolved. But now. In the very center of my hard story.

The door of the surgical ward finally opened. Just behind the attending nurse, Gary hobbled into the waiting room, a soft cast climbing halfway up his left calf. Relief surged through me like a tidal wave.

I darted toward him as tears spilled freely—this time, not from fear, but from pure joy and gratitude. Gary was still here. Whole. Alive.

He had also wrestled, imagining me in that cold, sterile waiting room—alone on an unfamiliar island, vulnerable and afraid. He had been powerless to shield me. Yet, I am convinced his prayers in that surgical room unleashed a miracle. All I knew was something had shifted—both in the room's atmosphere and in my own trembling mind. I couldn't wait to tell him what had happened—the way God intervened in my turmoil.

"Gary, it is all right. I wasn't alone."

And that's the truth—for all of us… though you may not yet feel that way. You are never alone. Not in sterile waiting rooms. Not in unfamiliar places. Not in the chaos, nor in the calm.

He promises to be right here—with you, offering A Place of Protection.

Sometimes It Takes a Shipwreck

Days after that experience, my thoughts kept returning to a familiar story—one I had read many times before, but now it felt so real.

I don't think many people in Scripture had more reason to fear than Paul. He was hunted for his faith, beaten, imprisoned, and eventually placed in chains aboard a ship bound for Rome. God had promised he would stand before Caesar—but the journey there was brutal.

Headwinds stalled the voyage. Then the storm came.

"A storm of hurricane strength raged for many days, blotting out the sun and the starts, until at last all hope was gone."
Acts 27:20 (NLT)

I lingered over that line: *all hope was gone.*

That felt familiar. I was comforted knowing Paul knew how that felt, too.

Paul wasn't spared the storm. He wasn't rescued early. He didn't control the outcome. And yet—somehow—he wasn't undone by it. I noticed what held him steady when everything else was stripped away:

"Last night an angel of the God to whom I belong and whom I serve stood beside me and said, 'Don't be afraid...'"

Acts 27:23-24 (NIV)

God stood beside him.

Not after the storm. Not once the ship reached shore. But in the middle of the chaos—when fear had every reason to raise its voice.

That was the connection I hadn't noticed before. God's protection didn't mean Paul avoided the shipwreck. It meant he wasn't *alone in it.*

The account is epic. The ship was totally obliterated, but every life was spared—just as God had promised. I imagine those 276 men never forgot that night. Not the wind. Not the waves. And not the God who met them there.

I can now recognize how often I longed to know God more deeply while quietly resisting the very circumstances that invite His nearness. But the two are rarely separate. Storms have a way of awakening our ears to His voice. They loosen our grip on certainty and draw us with longing for the shelter of His presence.

Much later, Paul would write words that came from experience… now, a deep place of confidence. All I could think of as I read them was the hope that he was offering me because of the power of God's faithfulness in his own testimony:

"He did rescue us from mortal danger, and He will rescue us again. We have placed our confidence in Him, And He will continue to rescue us."
2 Corinthians 1:10 (NLT)

I am beginning to believe that safety doesn't always look like rescue from the storm. I think most of the time, it looks like being held fast within it.

INVITING GOD TO BECOME YOUR PLACE OF PROTECTION

As I look back on these moments—the fear, the waiting, the safety I didn't know I needed I am reminded that God often invites us to slow down before He invites us to move forward.

Because Scripture was already deeply vital to me, I found great comfort in the promises embedded in the Bible. The pages ahead are a space for you to do the same. Not to fix what's broken, but to sit with the One who holds it. I invite you to meditate on God's Word, allowing it to steady you, gently and patiently, in whatever storm you find yourself.

What is Meditation: Sometimes we hear the word "meditation" and immediately picture emptying the mind or achieving a mental state. Biblical mediation is the opposite of that. It is not trying to stop thoughts. It is choosing one true thought and allowing it to slowly reshape all the others. It is choosing to think about God's word long enough to reach our hearts. This is how scripture moves from information to formation, shaping the way we think and how we process our circumstances.

Ways to Meditate on Each Passage:

1. **Ask God to speak.**

   Begin by praying: *"Father, what do You want to show me about Yourself? Where do You want to work in my heart today?"*

2. **Read slowly and repeatedly.**

   Go over the verse several times, emphasizing a different word or phrase each time. For example:

   *The **Lord*** is good...
   The Lord ***is*** good...
   The Lord is ***good***...

   (Continue slowly, letting each word invite deeper reflection.)

3. **Watch for what stands out.**

   Did a word or phrase tug at your heart? That may be the Holy Spirit highlighting something He wants to reveal.

4. **Notice resistance.**

   Did anything stir pain, doubt, or even frustration? Talk honestly with Jesus about it. He can handle your heart's deepest ache.

5. **Follow what brings anticipation.**

   Did a phrase stir confidence, hope, or peace? These are traces of His voice. Respond to what you sense He's saying.

6. **Pray honestly.**

   Your prayer might sound like:

   "Abba, I want to know You more. Teach me to rest in Your protection."
   If you keep seeking Him, He will keep revealing Himself to you. Lay your head on His chest. Listen to His heart.

7. **Carry it with you.**

   Write the verse on a notecard or sticky note. Place it where you'll see it throughout the day—on your mirror, dashboard, or on your phone. Let it re-center your thoughts.

There is no hurry here. Only an invitation to come and let God become *Your Place of Protection.*

Over the coming days, choose one passage at a time to sit with. Breathe deeply, inhaling God's peace, exhaling your fears. As you are able, allow these verses to become anchors, holding your storm-tossed soul. Don't rush. Linger in the words. Invite God to speak. Let His truth steady you.

Daily Scriptures to Anchor Your Soul

Day 1:

The LORD is good, a strong refuge when trouble comes.
He is close to those who trust in him.
—Nahum 1:7 (NLT)

Day 2:

Lord, I cry out to you.
I say, "You are my place of safety.
You are everything I need in this life."
—Psalm 142:5 (NIrV)

Day 3:

...my God is my rock, in whom I find protection.
He is my shield, the power that saves me,
and ***My Place*** *of safety.*
—Psalm 18:2b (NLT)

Day 4:

It is better to take refuge in the Lord
than to trust in people.
—Psalm 118:8 (NLT)

Day 5:

But you, O LORD, are a shield about me,
my glory, and the lifter of my head.
I cried aloud to the LORD,
and he answered me from his holy hill.
(Selah)
I lay down and slept;
I woke again, for the LORD sustained me.
Psalm 3:3-5 (ESV)

Day 6:

"I have not given you a spirit of fear,
but of power,
of love and of a sound mind."
2 Timothy 1:7 (NLT)

Day 7:

"There is no one like the God of Israel.
He rides across the heavens to help you,
across the skies in majestic splendor.
He is your protecting shield
and your triumphant sword!
Your enemies will cringe before you,
and you will stomp on their backs!"
Deuteronomy 33:26b (NLT)

My Prayer of Protection over all your fear:

Oh, Place of Protection, I long to know You as my Shelter in the storm, my Fortress when I am afraid, my Rock when hope slips and turmoil surrounds me.

Forgive me for the times I've doubted You—for the moments I've run to lesser things instead of running to You first.

Thank You for Your relentless mercy, for Your love that never quits, and for welcoming me into the safety of Your presence.

Here I am, Lord—alone and afraid, exposed and weary. I need the assurance of Your nearness. Hide me beneath the shadow of Your wings. The battle around me is fierce. The enemy's threats are real. Please show me You are close.

Let me hear Your voice and feel the comfort of Your goodness

Today, I turn my face to You—not my back. I yield my will to Yours. May only Your plans and purposes prevail in my life. Take this tangle of fear and sorrow—and in return, I receive You: my Surrounding Shield, my Mighty Fortress, my Everlasting Rock.

Your Word says You will never fail, and that Your love endures forever. Help me believe that—deep in my bones. Awaken me with Your steadfast love in the morning, and help me to rest in it each night.

Open my eyes to recognize the ways You are working in the moments of my day.

Open my ears to hear Your voice calling me: Beloved.

I give You my life today. Here I am—held, covered, and protected in Your everlasting arms. Amen.

Record your prayer.

When you're ready, write your own prayer to God. Use this space, or your favorite journal, to capture your heart's honest cry, your gratitude, or your questions.

SECTION SIX

The Place of Pardon

For All My Guilt

Even now my witness is in heaven;
my advocate is on high.
My intercessor is my friend
as my eyes pour out tears to God;
on behalf of a man he pleads with God
as one pleads for a friend.

Job 16:19-21 NIV

CHAPTER 16

WHEN GUILT WHISPERS LOUDLY

Therefore, there is now no condemnation
for those who are in Christ Jesus.
Romans 8:1(NIV)

A Do-Over

Have you ever longed for a do-over—the chance to change an outcome, rewind a moment of regret, take back a word, or repair a mistake?

To explore that longing more personally, allow me to step forward in our story--nearly a decade after Karissa's loss. God graciously entrusted us with more children—gifts we did not take lightly. We delighted in their unique personalities and celebrated their strengths. Our daughter Hannah, the oldest of our future four, was now a bright third grader—highly motivated, a voracious reader and intensely competitive.

When her school hosted a spelling bee, she set her sights high. She mastered every word on the third-grade list. Difficult words were not threats; they were challenges to conquer. Her diligence paid off—she would represent her school at the regional competition.

About sixteen students stood on stage as the announcer reviewed the rules: *"Say, the word. Spell the word and then say the word again so we know you have completed your spelling. You may ask me for a definition. You may start over—but you cannot change any letter once spoken."*

Round after arduous round passed. One by one, contestants took their seats. At last, only Hannah and one other boy remained.

Then came her next word: *"Your word is cowboy."*

She smiled at us in disbelief. After mastering words like *yacht*, *hierarchy*, and *conscientious*, this was a gift.

She began quickly—too quickly: *"Cowboy. C-O-U...* (pause)… C-O-W-B-0-Y."

Her eyes closed. Correction came too late. The rules were clear. Her heart deflated like a tire losing air as she exited the stage.

All attempts to cheer her up were futile. We reminded her how remarkable it was simply to reach regionals, but she didn't want perspective—she wanted a do-over.

We tried to pivot the day—ice cream, or another spontaneous outing. Her siblings were thrilled. Hannah was not. Some disappointments, no matter how small they appear, cling tightly to tender hearts.

For days she groaned, *"Cowboy? Who misspells cowboy?"*

Childhood setbacks may seem minor compared to adult failures, but they offer early rehearsals to extend grace to ourselves—grace when we miss the mark, gentleness when we hang our heads in shame.

Eventually, the sting faded. The story became safe enough to laugh about. But nearly three decades later, Hannah reflected on it differently. *"I never competed in another spelling bee after that,"* she said. *"I didn't realize how deeply that mistake must have deflated my confidence in something I loved."*

As I listened, I recognized how some failures evaporate. Others linger—quietly shaping how we see ourselves. What begins as a single misstep or bad decision can plant something deeper in the soil of the soul: shame, regret, insecurity and the belief that it's safer not to try again.

After Karissa's death, I understood the way choices had etched deep grooves into my own soul, how regret rehearsed itself until it felt permanent. Accusation slipped in, calling me names I would never speak… defining me by my worst moment.

As Henri Nouwen wrote, "*Self-rejection is the greatest enemy of the spiritual life because it contradicts the sacred Voice that calls us the 'Beloved.'* Our identity as '*Beloved'* constitutes the core truth of our existence."[xxv]

Not Your Defining Day

Shame had not marked my childhood. Regret was not a companion I knew in those early years. But after I lost Karissa, those emotions would nearly undo me.

As a child, my world was filled with awe and wonder. When I was ten years old, God's love reached into our dysfunctional family and began transforming every fractured corner of our lives. His grace felt tangible then — close, steady, unmistakable.

My alcoholic dad was set free from a generational addiction the night he surrendered his broken life to Jesus—at an Irish concert of all places. The singers presented the hope of the Gospel in a way that reached my dad's heart—for the first time. That evening, he surrendered his life to Jesus and, from that moment on, his life changed. He became what scripture calls a new creation in Christ. (2 Corinthians 5:17)

His angry, miserable soul softened into a gentle, loving—transformed father. This had a profound ripple effect on me, my mom and siblings who had tip-toed through decades of dysfunction. We were finding hope and purpose in our own growing relationship with Jesus.

I watched in amazement as our entire household was being renewed. I didn't just hear about the love of God—I *saw* it. I *felt* it. I embraced that love, and it embraced me. It was as if Jesus' grace was pouring over our home like healing oil. I was ruined for the ordinary. My life changed forever.

An elderly man taught us how to grow in this relationship with Jesus. By meditating on Scripture and learning how to talk to God, we discovered His desire to reveal Himself to us. I loved my new Bible. Whenever I opened God's Word, something happened: He spoke to me… through it. Though I was only a child, He seemed to enjoy revealing Himself to me. Many nights, my bedroom light stayed on, not because I was afraid of the dark, but because the light of His Word was flooding my soul with wonder and joy. I couldn't stop reading.

This wasn't just my parents' faith. God captured my desires and imagination. I decided then that He would be the foundation I built my life on. Storms would eventually come to threaten its strength, but His love had built something inside me I was confident could hold in any trial.

Yet somewhere between childhood wonder and adult grief, shame found its way in, and that foundation was put to the test when Karissa passed away.

My childhood faith had been built on rescue, transformation, protection, and intimacy with God. I witnessed His power when He set my dad free. I had felt His Word steady my young heart. I believed His love guarded whatever we entrusted to Him.

So, when tragedy struck, my theology had to reconcile two realities:

God is good.
My child is dead.

If both were true, something had to account for the fracture between them.

It was a rare day, two months after her death. I found myself in a strangely quiet house. For the first time, I was completely alone. My friends had other commitments. Gary was at the office—only ten minutes away. Still… it felt much too far.

I knew he'd be home in an instant if I called, but that morning, I didn't want to call. I wanted to prove to myself I could survive the silence.

I inhaled deeply—a shaky breath—and repeated one of my favorite Scriptures aloud, trying to steady my thoughts:

"I can do everything through Christ who gives me strength."
Philippians 4:13 (NLT)

Today, I wanted to remember what that felt like to function like an emotionally strong adult.

So, I made a list—my first in months. It was a manageable checklist for the next few hours: Wash dishes. Mop the floor. Fold laundry. Surprise Gary (if time allowed) with a loaf of freshly baked bread for lunch.

I pictured the sense of achievement I would feel when Gary arrived. This was a start—baby steps toward healing.

I carefully avoided the rooms that felt unbearable. The kitchen and laundry room felt safe enough and gave me plenty to do. I fixed my gaze forward at the sink window, letting the outside world widen my view beyond the hostile walls around me. Behind me loomed the entrance to Karissa's room. I refused to turn around.

But silence has a way of amplifying absence. As I scrubbed a pan with increasing force, the quiet pressed in. I should have turned on music, but it was too late. That would require walking through spaces I wasn't ready to face. The weight behind me grew heavier—until it seemed to collapse inward. Without warning, panic overwhelmed me.

What happened next did not come from the heart of God. It came from a wounded heart and a very real enemy who knows how to weaponize grief.

At first, the thoughts were faint. Then they sharpened.

What if you deserved this pain?
What if you had gone to Karissa sooner?
What if your love for her had quietly eclipsed your love for God?

The questions grew crueler.

You made her your idol.
You failed her.
You could have stopped this.

These thoughts didn't carry a speck of mercy. They carried the weight of condemnation. The enemy did not attack my belief in God's existence. He attacked my relationship within His love.

Frantic to escape the noise, I bolted out the side door into our detached garage where we kept the kittens. I gathered two playful bodies into my arms and pressed my face into their fur. Their tiny, steady heartbeats reminded me I was still alive.

But this war was not surrounding me. It was inside my mind.

If God was still good, perhaps I was not.
If He had not failed, perhaps I had.

The enemy twisted grief into indictment. He took unanswered questions and sharpened them into verdicts against me. Guilt became the wall he erected between what I believed about God and what had happened in my life.

And for a time, it felt almost reasonable.

Those initial accusations were the prelude to the crushing condemnation that followed. It seemed like every critical thought, vain imagination, prideful attitude, futile daydream, and selfish ambition rose to testify against me.

In that moment I cried out, "*Oh God, did the weight of all my sin lead to Karissa's death? Is her absence the result of my failures?*"

Unanswered questions. Unrelenting guilt. Unshakable fear. They paralyzed me.

I wanted to call Gary, but I was too afraid—afraid of walking back through the door toward more torment waiting inside. So, I stayed outside—on the cement steps by our kitchen—hoping for noon to arrive swiftly.

Time passed. Slowly, the sun's penetrating warmth began to calm my trembling frame. I felt the vibrating purr of the kittens, still in my arms. My anxious mind quieted. A melody of spring birds—this gentle brush of life around me—began to steady me. It was as if God was summoning nature itself to drown the vile charges screaming in my head.

In that stillness, I found strength to speak to my soul rather than listen to the accusations against it.

"*Patty... do you really believe these indictments?*

They didn't sound like the Voice I had come to know over the years. They didn't carry God's compassion. They didn't invite His healing. They were words of condemnation, declaring Karissa's death as deserved punishment. And I knew deep within, *that* didn't line up with everything I built my life on.

A favorite promise, memorized long before, surfaced. As if God, Himself, was running to my rescue, crushing the enemy's wall of false guilt. My Defender offered a lifeline to my tormented soul:

For as high as the heavens are above the earth,
so great is his love for those who fear him;
as far as the east is from the west,
so far has he removed our transgressions from us.
As a father has compassion on his children,
So, the Lord has compassion on those who fear him;
for he knows how we are formed,
he remembers that we are dust.
Psalm 103:11-14 (NIV)

As I sat there, those words of life secured me. This was the God I had known—the One full of compassion, swift to defend, ready to remove every residue of guilt, sin, and shame. His correction had always drawn me closer, never into despair. Whenever He confronted any form of sin in my life, it had always been with mercy. When He invited repentance, it brought hope and change.

I remembered another promise—one I had clung to many times before. One I desperately needed now:

If we confess our sins,
He is faithful and just to forgive us our sins
and to cleanse us from all wickedness.
1 John 1:9 (NLT)

Slowly, the truth settled in. The false accusations couldn't alter Truth or amend God's character. My grief had not canceled His grace. It revealed my need for it. Whatever else was happening inside me, this much was clear: the aching young mom on those steps was deeply loved by God.

And that's when I began to see it—my mind was not only wrestling with profound grief, but an enemy far more sinister, was exploiting my pain and turning it against me—into guilt. The accusations weren't leading me toward God. They were a vile attempt to pull me away from Him.

CHAPTER 17

THE ACCUSER UNMASKED

He was pierced for our transgressions,
and he was crushed for our iniquities.
The punishment that brought us peace was on him;
and by his stripes we are healed.
Isaiah 53:5 (NIV)

Certain facts surrounding Karissa's death carried a truth I couldn't deny. Simple changes could have changed the outcome for our family. I think many who grieve understand this line of reasoning—but it generally leaves us drowning in guilt and regret. *If only I had changed the flight... removed the blanket... gotten to the hospital sooner... awakened in time to answer her cries. If only...*

But I didn't have that kind of knowing. And yet the ache of those questions lingered.

Scripture reveals Satan's long history of mastering ways to exploit our pain and twist it into guilt. He whispers lies (often laced with truth) that stick like burrs to our soul: *It's too late. There's no hope. Life is over.* Those declarations root in our failures, shame, and regrets—until they become part of our identity.

Scripture gives a name to this voice of condemnation: the Accuser. He stands before God, day and night, hurling charges against us. He rages against mercy and despises Jesus' complete forgiveness.

In a recent reading of Job, the earliest book on suffering, I noticed accusation was woven throughout the story. Even Job's closest friends began to echo the Accuser's voice: suffering must be proof of guilt or a sign of God's disinterest.

I could feel those familiar accusations at work in my own story, trying to build a wall between me and the God I loved. The same voice that accused me before God, also whispered accusations about God to me:

How can you call Him good? If He loved you, wouldn't this have turned out differently?

It is a subtle strategy: When we begin to doubt God's goodness, it becomes difficult to rest in His love. And yet, no wall is so thick that God's love cannot break through it.

Job believed this in the middle of his unbearable story:

Even now my witness is in heaven;
my advocate is on high.
My intercessor is my friend
as my eyes pour out tears to God;
on behalf of a man he pleads with God
as one pleads for a friend.

Job 16:19-21 (NIV)

Job believed there was a God in heaven defending him—even when everything felt like evidence against him. There may be an accuser, but we have an Advocate: Jesus—our intercessor—the One who stands between accusation and those He loves, promising, *"nothing can ever separate us from God's love... not even the powers of hell."* (See Romans 8:38 NLT)

Those Satan accuses, God makes right—not by our effort, but by Christ's finished work on the cross. Slowly, I began to see that my worst day did not have to become my defining day.

As I write this, I can't help but think of those who may be reading from places of deep regret—perhaps from a prison cell, or perhaps from the quieter prison of your own home. Maybe your guilt isn't imagined. Maybe your choices truly contributed to your pain. If that's you, I want you to know this: You are not beyond His mercy or complete forgiveness. No life is so lost that God doesn't know how to reach us.

Scripture tells us:

God, in his grace, freely makes us right in his sight. He did this through Christ Jesus when he freed us from the penalty for our sins.
Romans 3:24 (NLT)

That promise (among many) has lightened my load of shame so many times in my own life. Perhaps it can lighten yours, too. It's the story of the Bible, beginning to end:

Compelled by love, Jesus put on flesh to carry our condemnation on His back. He became my substitute--your substitute—taking the punishment we deserved. He tore down that wall of separation that kept us from Himself, restoring what sin had fractured. He invites us into *The Place* where we are fully pardoned. In Him, we are given an unshakeable identity: Guiltless. Blameless. Shameless.

I think the first time I ever began to really grasp the vastness of God's love was the day I saw the ocean for the first time. I was a young adult from the Midwest, arriving in Oregon for college. I had never witnessed anything as immeasurable and glorious as that first look of the boundless ocean. It left me speechless. Wave after wave crashed against the rugged Oregon coastline. In awe, I dropped to my knees in the rough sand. Tears streamed down my face as the lyrics from an old hymn finally made sense:

Could we with ink the ocean fill,
And were the skies of parchment made,
Were every stalk on earth a quill,
And every man a scribe by trade;
To write the love of God above
Would drain the ocean dry;
Nor could the scroll contain the whole,
Though stretched from sky to sky.
~Meir Ben Isaac Nehorai (A.D.1050)[xxvi]

This image became a regular refrain during those battles against accusation. It has changed the way I look at every ocean. The seas declare the incomprehensible love of God. I knew I could never earn His favor. I also knew, through Jesus, I already had it. So, I could stand amid every accusing thought, knowing one thing was true of this undeserved grace: I was completely covered, fully accepted, and deeply loved.

So, I guess it doesn't matter what story we're in the middle of—even in the most broken situations—no condemnation hangs over us. None.

"Therefore, there is now no condemnation
for those who are in Christ Jesus."
Romans 8:1 (ESV)

Between Two Sinners

It was no accident that Jesus—the pure and spotless Lamb of God—hung on a cross between two criminals. As I pondered that scene, I couldn't imagine the agony and humiliation He endured. Slowly, I began to see those two men as representatives of all humanity—both guilty, condemned, and powerless to save themselves.

Yet there, between them, hung the One through whom mercy could be found—*The Place* where a fresh start was still possible.

One believed in this Man hanging between them. The other didn't.

One confessed his guilt and, in his final breath, reached toward hope. With nothing to offer the dying King, he turned toward Jesus: "*Will you remember me when you come into Your kingdom?"*

Will you remember me? These words sound offensive—it seemed too late for a thief to ask for mercy. He was a lawbreaker. He most likely never read Scripture—he certainly didn't regard it if he had. And yet, he had the audacity to whisper this unthinkable request? Is that the way to find life in *The Place of Pardon*? A simple turning toward Jesus? Asking to live in His presence?

Jesus replied, *"Today you will be with Me in paradise."* My translation: *"From this moment on, I'll never leave you or forsake you."* What the thief thought was the end of his life became the beginning of eternal life. When he thought he had reached the end of his story, Jesus entered it to give him hope and a future.

The other criminal, also facing imminent death, mocked The Redeemer and demanded proof of His Lordship. Even as he inched his way toward an eternity without God, he refused to admit his need for the Savior. He preferred to cling to his ruined life rather than offer it to the One willing to write him a new story.

Without favoritism, Jesus' arms stretched toward them both. He didn't demand explanations for their current state. He didn't lay out a list of requirements for entrance into heaven. In the shadow of Jesus' own suffering, He simply offered The Life He was dying to give them.

Jesus guaranteed the criminal a place with Him forever. He was made new and invited into an eternal relationship with God. This radical love and boundless forgiveness stretched in both directions—freely given. The choice was theirs—to receive it or not.

And it still reaches… to us.

If the enemy is crushing us under the weight of condemnation… Whether the guilt we carry is misplaced… or painfully accurate… the invitation remains the same: Rest in *The Place* where your sins are pardoned—*The Place* where your relationship with God is secure.

God's ears are always tuned to the audacious request: *Will you remember me?*

Where Mercy Met Me

That morning on the cement steps outside our kitchen—squirming kittens still playing in my lap and the air thick with accusation, I felt *The Place of Pardon* reaching toward me. Though I had no fight left for the battle that raged, His Word held me.

Gently, steadily, it dismantled the indictments that had felt so convincing only moments before. It lifted the crushing weight from my shoulders.

I began to trust something my soul had been too beaten to grasp: even accusations tangled with fragments of truth held no power to condemn me. They came too late. My sins—every one of them—had already been carried to the cross before I lived a single day.

My sin—our sin—the whole of it—was nailed there. We don't have to live under the weight of it any longer.

That morning was a turning point. I was learning how to answer accusation with truth, to steady myself in God's forgiveness, and rest in His love.

"I, even I, am he who blots out
your transgressions, for my own sake,
and remembers your sins no more.
Isaiah 43:25 (NIV)

I was finding my home within my *Place of Pardon*.

CHAPTER 18

BEYOND BLAME

You saw me before I was born.
Every day of my life was recorded in your book.
Every moment was laid out
before a single day had passed.
Psalm 139:16 (NLT)

Gary arrived home for lunch, shocked to find me on the stairs. He sat beside me as I recounted the battle—the accusations, the twittering birds sent to steady my heart, the quiet presence of the Holy Spirit, guiding me back to forgotten truth.

Tears streamed down Gary's face as he lifted mine. Together, we thanked God for meeting us in our suffering—for exchanging shame for the assurance of His love, for opening wide the doors of His heart to become *Our Place* of Pardon.

To call this event the final battle would be a dishonest telling of our story. Receiving pardon can settle the question of our guilt, but it doesn't always quiet our questions. The temptation to blame ourselves—or question God—would return.

We would still wrestle with His involvement on January eighth. With imagined realities where we woke sooner, removed a blanket, and rescued our girl.

It seems that even after condemnation loosened its grip, I longed to aim my fury somewhere. Loss demanded answers. Over time my questions shifted. I was no longer asking, *"am I forgiven?"* I was wondering, "*why did this happen at all?"*

I remember the disciples asking a similar question when they encountered a man born blind:

"Rabbi," his disciples asked him, "why was this man born blind?
Was it because of his own sins or his parents' sins?"
John 9:2 (NLT)

They assumed someone must have done something terribly wrong. I wondered the same thing: *"Who was to blame for Karissa's death?"* Surely Jesus knew the backstory of this blind man. But His answer surprised them:

"It was not because of his sins or his parents' sins," Jesus replied.
"This happened so the power of God could be seen in him."
John 9:3 (NLT)

I doubt they saw that answer coming. I know I didn't.

The relentless demand to solve the blame riddle is nearly universal. When pain enters the story, something in us longs to explain it—to identify a cause, to assign responsibility, to make sense of the ache. I began to see how easily that search can send us down twisted tracks of anger, resentment, or quiet hostility.

The hard truth is this: life and pain are inseparable. Jesus never promised to shield us from either—but He did promise He would never abandon us in the suffering when He forewarned:

In this world you will have trouble.
But take heart! I have overcome the world."
John 16:33b (NIV)

Jesus' own life was marked with suffering. He did not model a way to avoid it, but a way to walk through it. I felt gently challenged by a new question. Instead of asking, *"Who is to blame?"* something different slowly emerged: *"God, how do You want to reveal Yourself here—in this suffering?"*

The apostle James understood how suffering could distort our view of God. If we can't pin the guilt on someone else, we often pin it on Him:

God, You could have stopped this.

Do You even hear my prayers?

What's the use of praying if You are going to do what You want anyway?

The rising tides of suffering threaten our ability to trust God's goodness and involvement in our lives. These are honest tensions—ones I hated, ones I didn't speak, but God knew they were real. That may be why scripture urges suffering believers with such tenderness:

"Do not be deceived, my beloved brethren.
Every good gift and every perfect gift is from above,
and comes down from the Father of lights,
with whom there is no variation or shadow of turning."
James 1:16-17 (NIV)

Scripture doesn't minimize pain—but it anchors hearts. God remains the source of every good gift—always. His nature does not fluctuate with our circumstances, even when our understanding does. Suffering and tragedy are part of living in a sin-sick world. They touch believer and unbeliever, rich and poor, innocent and guilty alike.

"Do not be deceived," James warned. From the moment Adam and Eve believed the lie that God was holding out on them, deception entered the human story—and pain followed close behind.

When Adam sinned, sin entered the world.
Adam's sin brought death,
so death spread to everyone, for everyone sinned.
Romans 5:12 (NLT)

Yet, even in their rebellion, God sought them out—not to crush them, but to cover them. The hand that reached for them was a hand of mercy. And that same merciful hand still stretches to our deceived and hurting world.

I will never forget God's defense that morning—or how Gary lifted my eyes above the heartache. His words became an exhortation I would declare through the years: *"God is bigger than a blanket, Patty."*

And Gary was right. The tragedy that blindsided us did not surprise Him. His plans were not upended by our loss.

One of my favorite Psalms assures us of this:

"You saw me before I was born.
Every day of my life was recorded in your book.
Every moment was laid out
before a single day had passed.
Psalm 139:16 (NLT)

The pain and loss that catches us off-guard, does not surprise God. The blow that splits our lives into two volumes—*before and after*—was already known to Him.

Long before we lived a single day, He knew the details within the moment we were currently facing. He recorded every chapter of our story—including this one. And even now, He continues to write redemption over us. (See Psalm 56:8)

Maybe, like me, death or destruction has threatened to diminish your life. Maybe it feels as though everything you loved has been reduced to rubble. But tragedy does not get the final word. God does. It is His nature to bring light into our darkness; to comfort us in mourning, to exchange our ashes for beauty, and our despair for joy. (See Isaiah 61:2-3)

I believed Jesus had the power to change Karissa's story—and mine. And yet, He chose not to. Could I learn to trust His master plan in all of this? Could I trust He knew things I would never fully understand?

Instead of believing her life was cut short or extinguished before it blossomed, I anchored my faith to that promise that all Karissa's days had been written before one of them came to be. (see Psalm 139:16 NIV)

Last time I checked *all* meant every single one of those days. Almighty God scripted every detail of Karissa's story. He etched the details of mine. And He has penned the details of *your*s.

Karissa's life included six priceless months and twenty-eight irreplaceable days. I believe when she entered eternity, she heard the words, *"Well done my good and faithful servant. Come and share your master's happiness!"* (See Matthew 25:21 NLT)

The length of our days does not determine their meaning. Nor does it measure the work God accomplishes through them. If I could believe Karissa completed everything God sent her to do, perhaps I could also learn to trust that her brief appointment in my story held a greater purpose than I could currently comprehend.

I began to refuse the narratives that tried to name me—*poor*, *pitied*, or *doing okay under the circumstances*. Instead, I chose to believe that even here, God would receive glory through my story.

Though I couldn't imagine it during those raw, early years after Karissa's death, one day I would find author Lysa TerKeurst's words to be true:

"What if God wasn't 'picking on me' but was 'picking me out' for his great purposes? What if my suffering was not in vain but by design? Sometimes hardship happens, not because of what you've done but because of something God is doing."[xxvii]

INVITING GOD TO BECOME YOUR PLACE OF PARDON

Dear One,

Has the enemy used accusation, guilt, or shame to tether your soul to a painful past? The thief hanging on the tree reminds us of this simple hope-filled truth: when we ask, Jesus will forgive *anything* we allow Him to touch.

When I offered Him my life—every piece of my hard and broken story—a beautiful exchange took place. He offered me His life—limitless in love, boundless in power and healing grace.

Perhaps something deep within you longs to pause… maybe aches to pray but doesn't quite know how. The Holy Spirit is gentle. He longs to awaken your heart and give you both the desire and ability to receive God's love. Even now—especially now—He offers you the best gift possible: Himself.

And when the blows come for you—when the Enemy blinds your mind with interrogation lights, distorted images, or harsh questions, remember this:

Jesus is the Place of Pardon.

For every condemnation.

For every failure.

For every blame-filled word.

For every moment you wish you could undo.

Rest here—in Jesus' mercy and love.

God handles our wounded hearts with compassion:

He does not punish us for all our sins;
he does not deal harshly with us, as we deserve.
For his unfailing love toward those who fear him
is as great as the height of the heavens above the earth.
He has removed our sins as far from us
as the east is from the west.
The LORD is like a father to his children,
tender and compassionate to those who fear him.
For he knows how weak we are;
he remembers we are only dust.
Psalm 103:10-14 (NLT)

Perhaps you are just beginning a relationship with Jesus—or perhaps you are returning to Him again. I discovered coming to Him does not require a specific prayer or the perfect arrangement of words. Your prayer could be as simple as:

"Jesus, I give You my life,"

or

"Oh God, please come into my heart.
Forgive my sins.
Guide me in Your truth.
I need You."
Here is God's response:

"Come now, let's settle this," says the LORD.
"Though your sins are like scarlet,
I will make them as white a snow.
Though they are red like crimson,
I will make them as white as wool."
Isaiah 1:18 (NLT)

He invites you to come—as you are. He is your *Place of Pardon*—a place where you can live out the moments of your everyday life without condemnation, blame, or shame. In Christ, you are offered the same assurance the thief received that day.

Who then is the one who condemns? No one.
Christ Jesus who died—more than that,
who was raised to life—
is at the right hand of God and is also interceding for us.
Romans 8:34 (NIV)

As God strengthens your faith and meets you in this tender season, watch closely. Even now, a counter-narrative is being written over your pain—one shaped by grace, not shame.

An Anchor of Hope:

God's Place of Pardon is a safe place to abide. Read these words slowly. Let them settle.

You saw me before I was born.
Every day of my life was recorded in your book.
Every moment was laid out before a single day had passed.
Psalm 139:16 (NLT)

1. **Does a particular word or phrase draw your attention right now?**

   You don't need to analyze it—simply notice what your heart lingers over.

2. **What thoughts or emotions surface when you consider that nothing about your life has taken God by surprise?**

   There is no right or wrong response—only honesty.

3. **Is there a part of your story right now that feels especially tender or unresolved?**

   If so, you might gently place it before God, without needing answers yet.

Confronting The Lies:

From the position of '*the forgiven'*, consider the lies the Accuser has used against you.

1. Write down any lies you have believed:

2. Is there a truth that stood out to you from this section that counters the lie?

3. In prayer, lay each accusation at Jesus' feet. After you release them, you may want to declare the following promise over your soul:

   Who then will condemn me? No one—for Christ Jesus died for me and was raised to life for me, and he is sitting in the place of honor at God's right hand, pleading for me. Romans 8:34 (personalized)

Receiving Freedom:

Be encouraged. When your heart feels beaten down, Christ, Himself, continues to plead for you. His hand of mercy reaches into your pit and pulls you out.

Describe what it means that Jesus calls you *Forgiven and Beloved.*

A simple prayer:

Oh, God of all forgiveness,

I come to You battered and pierced by the lies of the enemy against me. He declares me 'fallen', but You call me 'Forgiven'.

He whispers shame, but You call me 'Sanctified'.

He casts blame, but You call me 'Beloved'.

I grip hold of Your hand of mercy, reaching for me.
I embrace Your cleansing sacrifice on the cross and declare, "You have made me white as snow."

You see my affliction and take it in hand. I place it in Your hands and ask for Your love in me to become stronger than any anger or hate in me. For You have poured out Your love into my heart through the Holy Spirit (from Romans 5:5). I receive that love.

Please, help me live in You—My Place of Pardon.

Amen.

SECTION SEVEN

The Place of Perspective

For All My Perplexity

But those who trust in the Lord
will find new strength.
They will soar high on wings like eagles.
They will run and not grow weary.
They will walk and not faint.

Isaiah 40:31 NLT

CHAPTER 19

CLIMBING HIGHER

"Open my eyes to see the wonderful truths in your instructions. I weep with sorrow; encourage me by your word."
Psalm 119:18, 28 (NLT)

It's Pretty Hazy Down Here

Grown up life is a lot more perplexing than I imagined it would be. As a child I considered myself an expert in human reasoning. Life felt linear—right and wrong, cause and effect, effort and outcome, all paired together neatly. Touch a hot stove? Get burned. Cut off your friend's ponytail? Big trouble—and a likely end to the friendship. Try to walk your pet turtle on a leash—only to discover when the limbs retract, its shell cracks. (Who would do a thing like that? Don't judge. I was only five.)

But it didn't take long before life outwitted my "expert" status. Somewhere along the way, the path grew foggy. Loss, disappointment, and unanswered prayers blurred the edges of what once felt clear.

Pain has a way of narrowing our vision. When grief enters the room, it presses in, filling the frame until it's hard to see anything else. The future feels uncertain. God can feel distant. And perspective—the ability to see beyond what hurts right now—feels painfully out of reach.

I've learned that this struggle isn't a sign of weak faith; it's a human response to suffering: Health fails. A co-worker belittles. A friend betrays our confidence. A spouse breaks vows. When this ground beneath us shifts, clarity doesn't come easily. We don't lose our desire to see—we lose our vantage point.

There are seasons when a fog rolls in over the landscape of our heartbreak—thick, relentless, and disorienting. We struggle to see ourselves or those around us… we squint, trying to see God. *Why isn't He involved in our struggle—moved by our suffering?*

We hope there's more beyond this fog, but from where we stand, all we can see is what's immediately in front of us. Sometimes, that's all pain allows.

From our view, wrong conclusions feel true. If left unchallenged, every trial, fractured relationship, and sorrow begins to warp our perspective of God.

It's About Time

The Lord is not slow in keeping his promise,
as some understand slowness.
Instead, he is patient with you,
not wanting anyone to perish,
but everyone to come to repentance.
2 Peter 3:9 NIV

Waiting has a way of unsettling us. Especially when we are hurting. Especially when the need feels urgent. God's timing can feel confusing—sometimes even cruel—when we are standing inside the ache.

In the Gospels, Jesus is never in a hurry. That truth has both comforted me and undone me.

Mary and Martha knew exactly who to call when their brother became gravely ill. They saw Jesus open blind eyes, heal lepers, restore the lame, and feed thousands with a few loaves and a couple fish. This was their 9-1-1 call—their desperate plea for help. They trusted His power completely.

But Jesus didn't come.

The Healer's timing seemed disastrously off. Days passed. Hope thinned. And before help arrived, their brother died.

I can only imagine the anguish of those hours—the waiting, the watching, the questions that must have surfaced as Jesus stayed away. We'll return to their story later. For now, it is enough to sit in the tension they carried—the pain of knowing Jesus could have stopped it—and not understanding His delay.

Years after Karissa's death, that same tension showed up in our home. Our son, Kolton, almost three years older than his baby brother, slept alone on the top bunk in a room clearly designed for two. One day, that room would hold whispered conversations, shared secrets, and the quiet comfort of sleeping in the same room. But right now, the empty lower bunk was unbearable.

Briley still slept in the nursery, all the way down the hall.

As Briley grew and began to "play" with his older brother, Kolton's daily question emerged:

"Can Briley sleep with me now?"

And each day, the answer was the same. *"Not yet, buddy. He'll grow up soon. Right now, he still wakes up at night. He's too small for a bunk bed."*

This question continued… for months. And day after day, the answer remained the same.

Then, one day, without even posing the question, Kolton stomped his foot, pointed at his brother, and declared, *"It's taking him a long time to grow up."*

From Kolton's limited perspective, it looked like his brother simply refused to grow—and like we were the ones delaying his dream. What he couldn't see were the reasons shaping our decision. They were shaped by factors beyond Kolton's grasp.

I get it. I don't have much patience either. I can't number the times I had grown exasperated with God's timing; certain *His* strategy was flawed. I've felt the sting of waiting when relief felt overdue, when my carefully laid plans unraveled, when answers didn't come fast enough to make sense of the pain.

Over time, I've learned—slowly, imperfectly—that part of spiritual maturity is admitting how limited my perspective really is. I see only what's in front of me. God sees what's forming beyond it.

He sees with omniscience—holding past, present, and future together in perfect clarity. He understands how every piece of life's puzzle fits into place. Sometimes all I hold in my hands is a single, random piece—just enough to stabilize the wobbly table leg of faith.

But time proves Him trustworthy. Just as I would finally tuck baby brother into Kolton's long-awaited bunk bed—God, also, proves trustworthy at the right time.

In Search of a Better View

I'm no bird expert, but decades ago, I became fascinated by eagles—mostly because of their physiology and what it represents spiritually. Though an eagle's hooked beak and powerful talons make it a fierce hunter, an eagle's greatest advantage is its vision—it can spot a rabbit from three miles away.[xxviii] To put that into perspective, with an eagle's vision, we would be able to read the date on a quarter from across a football field. Apparently, God designed their vision to increase in clarity, not by flying faster but by flying higher.

Scripture offers an invitation:

Those who hope in the LORD will renew their strength.
They will soar on wings like eagles.
Isaiah 40:31 (NIV)

I've often wondered what it means to soar, to "climb higher" when life feels heavy—when strength is scarce and answers feel elusive. What does it look like to set our gaze higher while standing in the thick fog of perplexing circumstances?

Author Mark Batterson writes, *"God has a three-hundred-and-sixty-degree perspective on everything... He sees all the way around everything—every issue, every person, every experience, every problem."*[xxix] Sometimes I forget that.

What if, instead of straining to make sense of life—and God—from our ground-level, foggy vantage point, we chose to climb higher—to draw closer—and asked Him to help us see with His unblocked perspective?

The story of Zacchaeus offers a glimpse of what might result from that climb.

A Worthwhile Climb

Zacchaeus was one of my favorite Sunday school characters. His name was fun to say... and in his culture, that name carried weight. *Zacchaeus* means innocent and pure. I can only imagine his parents' dreams—and maybe their prayers—for their boy: that he would be pure in heart and would lead an innocent life. Yet, that's not how his story played out.

Zacchaeus was a short-statured, chief tax collector for Rome. He had grown wealthy through threats, mistreatment, and oppression.

Yet, when he heard Jesus was coming into town, he set his work aside. Too short to see over the crowd and too despised to be welcomed into it, he found himself on the outside—longing for a glimpse of Jesus.

He did the only thing he could think to do: he climbed. Not to be seen—but to see.

He didn't climb because it was dignified or impressive. He climbed because something in him needed a different perspective. From the ground, all he could see were backs and shoulders and rejection.

From the tree, he hoped—simply hoped—he might catch sight of the One he'd heard could change everything. Rumor had it Jesus hung out with tax collectors and disreputable sinners like himself.

That curiosity—and maybe a deeper longing that only Jesus could see—drove him up that tree.

Zacchaeus didn't know what He would find. He only knew he couldn't stay where he was. And so, he climbed—reaching above his limitations, above the pain and rejection he deserved, waiting to see the One who had somehow changed people like himself.

When Jesus entered the town, He walked straight toward the very one who wondered if he was beyond the reach of grace. Looking up into the tree, Jesus called him by name. Can you imagine Zacchaeus's shock? *"How do you know me? Who gave You my name?"*

In that sycamore tree Zacchaeus stood face to face with the One who could make sense out of his disordered life—the only One who could redeem his past and rewrite his future.

Then, Jesus did the unthinkable: He invited himself over to Zacchaeus's house for lunch. Scripture doesn't tell us what they talked about over their plate of fish and chips, but I doubt it was a lecture about his wretched life. Transformation rarely comes through condemnation. More likely, it came through experiencing Jesus' undeserved love and boundless grace.

By the time Zacchaeus cleared the table, he saw life with a new set of eyes. His vision cleared. He wasn't beyond the reach of a Savior willing to forgive his sin and empower him to live differently. His world shifted from the inside out:

Zacchaeus stood before the Lord and said,
"I will give half my wealth to the poor, Lord, and if I have cheated people on their taxes, I will give them back four times as much!"
Luke 19:8 (NLT)

Grace changed him. Grace changes us. The man who gouged now gave—above and beyond what he had stolen. I began to see how grace was slowly changing me, too. The young mom consumed in dark grief was beginning to see a glimmer of hope.

Maybe, you feel a bit like Zacchaeus, carrying pain no one sees. Maybe you are not even sure what you need, but you long for change. Take heart—Jesus sees you. He sees your desperate soul reaching for a branch, straining for a glimpse—and He calls *you* by name.

Jesus said He didn't come for the healthy. He came for us who realize we are sick. This story reminds me Jesus doesn't just open blind eyes or straighten crippled limbs. He welcomes busted and broken hearts to come out of hiding—and renews their vision in *The Place* of Perspective.

CHAPTER 20

WHEN GOD STOOPS LOW

The Lord is close to the brokenhearted;
he rescues those whose spirits are crushed.
The righteous person faces many troubles,
but the Lord comes to the rescue each time.
Psalm 34:18-19 (NLT)

I have felt like Zacchaeus. I wasn't collecting taxes or mistreating widows, but an internal bleed of doubt and confusion weakened me. Four months after Karissa's death, while friends were applauding my fierce devotion to God, I still longed for answers to the relentless questions that haunted me day after day.

Mother's Day was approaching. I was beginning to understand how days of celebration could become painful triggers—especially for those who no longer "qualified" for the occasion or who had been denied its joy after years of trying. Holidays expose the ache we work so hard to hide.

Anticipatory grief often cuts deeper than the grief we experience when the day arrives. My first Mother's Day was no exception. I tried to picture myself participating in our church's festivities: the parade of moms, the applause, the gift of a single white, pink, or turquoise carnation, and the prayer of blessing.

Twenty-five of us had become first-time moms within the past twelve months. Every new mom would stand on the platform. Was I expected to join them? I still felt like a mom, but a shattered heart and an album of still-life photos were the only fragments left of a title I once bore. Author Levi Lusko describes the dilemma well:

> *A child who loses his parents is called an orphan. One who loses a spouse is called a widow or widower, but what do you call a parent who has lost her only child? There is no title—for there are no words to describe something so unthinkable!*[xxx]

The past four months had already generated enough sympathy for a lifetime. I couldn't imagine a more depressing way to mark my first Mother's Day than standing as the object of sympathy in the "mom-parade," talk about the elephant in the room.

So, we chose to spend the day away from the crowd. A few quiet hours in nature would provide space to grieve and remember. We could lament the small things we didn't talk about—the milestones we would never see: Karissa's first words. *Mama, Daddy*. Her first steps. Her words forming into sentences. Her tiny tooth popping through, then one day wiggling free. Learning to skip, ride a bike, read, sing, and dance… one day growing into a young woman with a family of her own.

The idea of exposing our unfiltered emotions felt meaningful. But as a part of the church's ministry team, we needed our pastor's approval to miss this major holiday. I was sure he would understand our pain.

To our surprise, he denied our request. His reasoning gouged like a knife: "*Patty, you can't run from your grief forever. You'll never outrun it. You need to lean into the emotions of this day. Allow your church family to love and surround you.*"

Lean into it? His words sent a rush of panic and fury through me. Hadn't I been leaning into the crush of this reality for months? As we drove away from the meeting, I thought I might drown in the tide of tears swelling inside me.

I asked Gary to drop me off at the park near our home. The moment I reached the base of a random oak tree, the floodgates opened. Wordless agony poured out before the One I desperately needed to make sense of the storm raging inside me. I think He heard something like, "*Will this pain ever stop? I'm not sure I can survive this life without Karissa in it.*"

When the sobs finally subsided, I needed God to speak. So… I reached for my Bible, and let it fall open. Not exactly a recommended reading plan—but honestly, I had no plan. I'm pretty sure my lack of discipline didn't frustrate or disturb God. He didn't wait for me to employ a certain set of spiritual disciplines before He drew near. As unimpressive as my action appeared, I'm convinced God noticed a desperate girl reaching for a branch, climbing… yearning for a glimpse of His face above the chaos of her existence.

The page that opened before me held these words:

> *So, we are always confident, knowing that while we are at home in the body, we are absent from the Lord. For we walk by faith, not by sight. We are confident, yes, well pleased rather to be absent from the body and to be present with the Lord.*
> *2 Corinthians 5:6-8 (NKJV)*

Of all the passages I could have landed on, this one mattered. The opening phrase struck me: *"So we are always confident…"* How long had it been since that word described me?

Paul reminds us of our carnal limitations when it comes to human interaction with the Divine. Death is not an ending—it is the mysterious transformation from a fragile body into a heavenly one, a promise to those who love Jesus—an invitation into the fullness of His presence and glory forever.

This was the truth Jesus had affirmed to the criminal hanging beside him. *"I assure you, today (*not someday) *you will be with me in paradise."*

The Word of God searched my weary faith. He knew my soul was too broken to be bold, too crushed to feel confident. While harboring personal questions about death, about heaven—questions that vehemently rejected neat and tidy, one-size-fits-all answers, God listened to my darkest fears and deepest perplexities—to questions I was too ashamed to voice.

Where was Karissa...really? Was she asleep in the cold earth, waiting for the day she would finally be with Jesus at His great second coming? Or was she alive in His presence, fully loved... fully whole?

Her simple white casket was buried on top of a hill. At times, the thought of this beautiful child I held, nursed, and adored—now hidden in the ground—tormented my soul with an anguish too heavy to bear. I longed to trust that Karissa was not imprisoned by death but welcomed into resurrection life in Jesus' presence.

I opened my journal—its pages filled with a tangle of theological questions, still beyond my understanding. Slowly, I wrote the passage at the top of my page:

We are confident, yes, well pleased rather to be absent from the body and to be present with the Lord.

With pen in hand, I approached the Father with the kind of childlike faith Jesus invites us to embrace, carrying with me a load of questions that refused neat answers. I continued to write out my prayer:

Father, Your Word says that to be absent from this body is to be present with You. The last time I saw her; she was absent from her body. If I understand this passage correctly—then Karissa is with You—right now—in Your presence.

And if she is in your presence, may I ask you to do something for me? My arms ache to hold her. Would you gather her into your everlasting arms and hold her for me? And—I can no longer talk to her. But you can. Could you tell her how much her mommy still loves her?

It was as if the gloom-clouds of doubt, hanging over my days, lost density in God's presence. Courage welled up, and I decided to unleash one final request.

Oh God... just one more thing. Would you look into Karissa's crystal-blue eyes, kiss her sweet lips, and tell her that kiss was from her mommy?[xxxi]

There it was—the most audacious request I had prayed since her funeral. I leaned against the tree in utter silence, my heart laid bare—nothing hidden—before God. Nothing in my circumstances had changed. I was still expected to participate in the Mother's Day celebration. I was still living in the same world of suffering and heartbreak. Yet, within me, something had shifted: I was infused with the genuine hope of Christ's resurrection.

I felt completely heard and held by God. Tears, mingling with the ink in my journal, blurring words and clearing my vision at the same time. Against the solid bark of that old oak, I encountered *The Place of Perspective.*

He held my perplexed and broken heart. He entered my pain the same way He entered Zacchaeus' house—transforming yet another broken story. He lifted the crush of suffering from my shoulders and gave me the courage to trust Him with an unknown future.

I believed the psalmists words:

"You keep track of all my sorrows.
You have collected all my tears in your bottle.
You have recorded each one in your book."
Psalm 56:8 (NLT)

My husband loves me deeply and empathizes with my tears; but I guarantee you, he's not awake at night recording the contents of each one in his journal. But God records them—every single one. No tear slips past His notice. That knowledge stirred a desire to spend the moments of my life in His perfect love.

Climbing higher to see more clearly has little to do with one's ability to ascend—and everything to do with the posture of the searching heart.

A broken and a contrite heart God will never despise.
Psalm 51:17 (KJV)

Though I was too weak to comprehend the eternal nature of Karissa's life, I was carried on eagle's wings, drawn closer to God—by God himself. There, He allowed me to catch a glimpse of reality as He sees it.

I carried you on eagles' wings and brought you to myself.
Exodus 19:4b (NIV)

We will all face days when we feel too broken to approach Him, when the climb feels impossible. In those moments, He doesn't turn away when our tears pour out like a river. He will lift us up—onto His strong, competent wings and will carry us to Himself. He will clear our blurred vision. Beloved, we do not need to be strong—He is strong.

CHAPTER 21

CARRIED TO THE TABLE

Satisfy us each morning with your unfailing love,
so we may sing for joy to the end of our lives.
Give us gladness in proportion to our former misery!
Replace the evil years with good.
Psalm 90:14-15 (NLT)

Carried To the Table

That day under the oak tree, I discovered *The Place of Perspective*—the God who reaches for us when we don't have strength to reach for Him. His desire doesn't end with lifting us above despair. He longs to carry us into His presence, to give us a place at His table. Scripture offers a picture of belonging through the life of Mephibosheth.

He was a disabled man—a representation of those crippled by the tragedies of life. As a small child, his nanny was carrying him to safety after his father, Prince Jonathan, and grandfather, the famous King Saul, were killed in battle. While fleeing to spare his life, she stumbled and dropped him, leaving him crippled in both feet. The death of the king and prince left young Mephibosheth as a living heir in Saul's family. Relatives, desperate for a claim to the throne, sought to kill Jonathan's heir. Though his nanny rescued his life, the fall forever changed the condition of it.

Time passed, and Israel's mighty warrior, David—God's chosen king—took the throne. In those days, it was customary for a new dynasty to massacre anyone connected to the prior dynasty. But

Prince Jonathan was David's closest friend. David had promised Jonathan he would always extend kindness to his family. So, he asked if anyone knew of a living heir.

Enter Mephibosheth. After King David received news of Jonathan's son, he invited him into his palace. This crippled man not only received an introduction to the king—he was carried to David's table day after day. He lived in the palace, shared every meal with the King, and received an inheritance as the son of a former king. David treated him like family. He didn't earn that place at the table. He was carried there—again and again.

I felt like Mephibosheth under that oak tree. A fall left me crippled in both feet. Too broken to stand, too maimed to walk, I lacked the strength to pursue God. I could only see a withering life before me—until God reached for me. He carried my broken soul to His table. He nourished me and gave me a place of undeserved privilege in His presence. He called me his own.

Gratitude and joy overflowed the banks of my heart, filling it with true worship.

The young woman who jogged home that afternoon hardly resembled the hopeless one who had stumbled from the car in anguish. *The Place of Perspective* revived me and offered me a quiet assurance: Karissa lived in His presence. I had reason to celebrate on Mother's Day: I would rejoice in her resurrected life *through Christ.*

The Gospel and Basic Math

In grief, everything begins to feel like loss. Subtraction—not addition. Life seems to hold less love. Less future. Less meaning."

I think Jesus' cross felt like loss for Jesus' followers. For them, everything came to a screeching halt when He was crucified. The cross seemed to erase their very purpose. His death crushed the hope of those whose future was bound to His.

The Gospel of Luke tells the story of two of those followers who could no longer bear the weight of their shattered hope. With their back to Jerusalem, they trudged home to Emmaus, carrying perplexed hearts, shriveled joy, and remnants of the old life they knew before Christ.

They couldn't shake the image of that torturous cross. *Why did everything have to change*? Many of us can identify with those two despondent disciples—our backs turned on a promise so dear to us, our faces downward, piecing together fragments of our former reality.

That was how I felt the day my counselor pulled a cross out of his desk drawer and asked me what I saw.

A cross. (I enjoyed when he began the session with a simple question.)

"What shape does it resemble?"

A little too brightly, I answered. *An addition sign?* (I could play this game the entire hour.)

Nodding, he held the cross in his hand and put a tube in mine. When he asked me to look at the cross through its narrow view, I lost sight of the vertical beam. All that remained was the shorter, horizontal beam—*Now what do you see*?

Sticking with the theme, I deduced: *A subtraction sign?*

The counselor explained how Jesus followers could only view Jesus' suffering as subtraction. Loss. Death. The end of miracles. Lost identity. Perhaps this is how we view our own suffering.

But what if Jesus' work on the cross changed that notion? What if subtraction isn't the final impact of suffering? What if its impact does not diminish life, demolish purpose, or drain our hope?

The counselor asked me to drop the funnel, and my perspective changed again. The final outcome of the cross was never a subtraction sign. In full view, its shape favored an addition sign. It was beginning to make sense.

Golgotha was never the end. The cross, etched into the skyline, was the symbol of eternal addition in God's Kingdom. At the very place of death, new life was secured. At the Place of the Skull, eternal hope was born.

The author of Hebrews urges us to fix our eyes on Jesus, reminding us of *His view* of the cross: "*...for the joy set before him, he endured the cross.*" (see Hebrews 12:2) Jesus endured the beatings and brutal death, knowing it would become the catalyst for our addition into His Kingdom.

As I sat in that small office, I could feel the tears building. I recognized the work of addition still taking place—in me. The cross carries healing for those who trust Him, forgiveness for those who receive Him, and a future for those who lay their pain and shame at His feet.

The canyon dividing man from God was closed on the cross, while the thick temple curtain—separating God from His people—was split from top to bottom. The separation was over. The invitation extended to all—even to those crippled by life, who would need to be carried there.

John Stott once wrote, *"I could never myself believe in God if it were not for the cross. In the real world of pain, how could one worship a God who was immune to it?"*[xxxii]

The cross adds to our faith. It proves that Jesus is not immune to suffering, and He joins us in ours. He can create something good from our suffering in the same way He forged eternal good from His own.

The two followers headed toward Emmaus were certain Jesus' crucifixion ended all hope. Sadness shadowed their faces. As they walked, a stranger joined them. When he asked them what they were talking about, they were shocked.

What was everyone talking about? He must be the only person in the region who hadn't heard what happened to Jesus.

Yet they shared the reason for their grief. When he saw their hearts, broken with doubt and disbelief, He gently walked them through the scriptures, outlining all that had been written about Himself. He connected the details of His death to everything the prophets had written about the Messiah.

By the time they reached their village, a faint ember flickered in their hearts. They urged Him to stay. They didn't really need to. He had no intention of leaving them in their grief. At the dinner table He broke bread, blessed it, and handed it to them. In that moment, their eyes were open.

JESUS.

Then, as suddenly as He had appeared, He disappeared—but not before setting their hearts on fire. They wasted no time. Running all the way back to Jerusalem, they proclaimed the good news to Jesus' other followers: hope was restored, perspective renewed.

Dear One, Jesus is a lot closer than we think on every desolate road. He continues to seek out the despondent. His words still spark the embers in our souls. The resurrection doesn't promise a suffering-free life, but it guarantees new life. Suffering doesn't have to subtract.

Jesus can produce something imperishable from the very circumstances that threaten to diminish us. He will transform the ugliest situations into something profoundly beautiful when invited into our broken stories. That is the power of the Gospel. That is the good news that meets us wherever we wander, creating wind so a fire in our hearts may ignite.

INVITING GOD TO BECOME YOUR PLACE OF PERSPECTIVE

Beloved, the same Jesus who called Zacchaeus down from a tree, who stooped low to sit with me beneath my own oak of grief, and who walked patiently beside two weary friends on the Emmaus Road—still seeks out hurting hearts today.

He has not overlooked your suffering. He has not hurried past your questions. He longs to meet you where you are and gently carry you into His perspective.

Take a moment to breathe. There is no rush here.

Listen for What Stirred

As you finish this section, what story, image, or truth lingered with you most? What seemed to rise to the surface of your heart?

Write freely. There are no right answers.

Notice His Nearness

Looking back over your own journey, where have you glimpsed Jesus walking with you—through Scripture, through another person, in community, or perhaps in a quiet moment you didn't expect?

If you haven't sensed His nearness, you are not alone—and you are not failing. Perspective often comes slowly, like the gentle light at dawn.

Philippians 4:6 invites us to bring *everything* to Him—the questions, the ache, the longing, the unfinished prayers.

What is your *big ask* right now?

What feels unresolved, confusing, or heavy?

Gently invite Jesus into this place. Ask Him to become **your Place of Perspective**—not to explain everything, but to remain near, to steady your heart, and to help you see what you cannot yet discern.

AN ANCHOR OF HELP

"In all their suffering, He also suffered,
and He personally rescued them.
In his love and mercy, he redeemed them.
He lifted them up and carried them
through all the years."
Isaiah 63:9 (NLT)

Read these words slowly. Is there a phrase that caught your attention? Let it settle into your soul as you simply breathe.

You may want to grab your journal to pour out what your heart still carries. Not one tear escapes His notice; every longing, every question is safe in His hands.

A PRAYER FROM THE PERPLEXED HEART

The people believed,
and when they heard that the LORD had paid attention to them
and that he had seen their misery,
they knelt low and worshiped.
Exodus 4:31 (CSB)

O Father, more than anything, I long to believe You see me—that You are paying attention to the ache of my heart.

Assure me I am not alone on this desolate road. Just as You once stooped low to notice the misery of Your people, stoop low to me. Spark hope in these smoldering embers.

Transform my perplexed heart the way You transformed Zacchaeus, the travelers on the Emmaus Road, and countless others who have encountered You along the way.

O Place of Perspective, help me see You at work—even in this hard story. Meet me in the ordinary moments when this endless feeling of loss overwhelms.

Burn away the haze of confusion and light a fire in my soul that burns… with worship, joy, and restored vision. Carry me until I can stand again.

I open my heart to You today, and trust You to be my Place of Perspective.

In Your Holy Name I pray.

Amen.

SECTION EIGHT

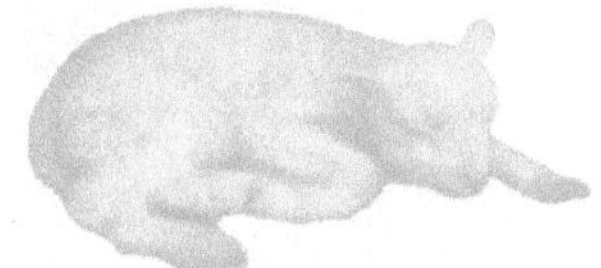

The Place of Promise

For All My Longing

"Yes, my soul, find rest in God;
my hope comes from him."

Psalm 62:5 NIV

CHAPTER 22

I SAW YOU

For he has not ignored or belittled the
Suffering of the needy. He has not turned His back on them,
but has listened to their cries for help.
Psalm 22:24 (NLT)

When Our Eyes Open

In the long months after Karissa's death, I realized how much it mattered to hear her name—I loved knowing she was remembered. In a way, it made me feel like I was still seen within grief's lonely landscape.

We had chosen Karissa's name long before we knew I would ever bear a child. Karissa's name described God's grace. When I became pregnant, we scanned name books in the event the baby was a boy or another name for a girl caught our attention. Names carry weight. They hold memories, meaning, and story. Some represent lives of faithfulness or courage.

Names, like fashion, cycle back into style. Today's classrooms are full of children with vintage names from the early twentieth century: Milly, Georgia, Esther, Molly, Amelia, Henry, Ernest, Jack, Charlie, and Frankie. It makes me wonder—when will names from the '60s make a comeback? I don't know many children named Patty, Barbara, Lisa, Renee, Monica, Sandy, Brian, Ken, Gary, or Scott. (If you're out there—your parents are ahead of the curve.)

Some names disappear for good. I've never met a guy named Ichabod. Nor a girl named Jezebel. Hagar is another name that didn't seem to rebound, but her name and her story would hold special meaning to me.

One day while reading the Bible, with eyes still clouded by grief, I encountered Hagar's story in Genesis. She was a servant to Abraham's wife, Sarah. Sarah longed for a child, but she was barren, so she offered her servant to Abraham, hoping to produce an heir through her.

Though this was not an uncommon practice in ancient times, it doesn't take a psychology degree to guess how this arrangement turned out. Once pregnant, Sarah and Hagar's relationship became unbearable. Hagar fled into the wilderness.

The Lord found her there and spoke to her. She was to return to her mistress. He told Hagar she was carrying a son and instructed her to name him Ishmael, meaning *the Lord hears.* His name would be a reminder: God hears the cry of the desperate—no matter their circumstances. Hagar gave God a new name that day: *You are the God Who Sees me.*

Sadly, this would not be Hagar's final wilderness journey. Years later, her conflict with Sarah was so great, she was banished to the wilderness for good— with a child and no clear future.

I've seen a Middle East wilderness. Protection from the intense sun and merciless wind is scarce in this wide-open landscape. Water—nearly nonexistent in that place. Hagar's rations didn't last long.

Scripture says Hagar wandered aimlessly. When her supplies ran out, so did her hope. Totally dehydrated, young Ishmael was nearing death. She laid him under a bush and walked away. She couldn't bear to watch him die.

The total abandonment in this scene is devastating: The boy's father didn't fight for him. A mother, too broken, fled from sight.

Alone and afraid, this child begins to cry. Ishmael's cry wasn't strong. It rose from a parched throat in a dry place, more of a desperate breath than a voice. Yet Scripture tells us that God heard the boy. *The God who hears* didn't miss it. *The God who sees* didn't overlook the mother collapsed in grief nearby. He was present in their wilderness—attentive, responsive, and moved with compassion.

God did not erase the wilderness. He gently moved into the hardship of that moment. Then He opened Hagar's eyes so she could see what had been there all along—a well of water within reach. Provision did not fall from the sky; it was revealed. Hope didn't arrive as rescue *from* the desert, but as sustenance *within* it.

Centuries later, this same God would draw even nearer. *The God who hears and sees* would take on flesh and dwell among us. In Jesus, God stepped fully into humanity's wilderness—listening to our cries, touching our wounds, and offering Living Water to those parched by grief and loss. Jesus didn't promise an escape from suffering, but He offered to be *Our Place of Promise* within it.

He remains the same God today—the One who hears the cries we can barely form and helps us see what we cannot yet recognize. In the wilderness, our story isn't over. God is still near. And sometimes, everything changes—not because the desert disappears, but because God opens our eyes.

Hopeless stories can be rewritten, and barren places can overflow with life.

I Saw You

I wish I could say I always recognized God's nearness after Karissa died. I didn't. Most days I felt like Hagar—trying to manage unbearable loss with limited strength and even fewer answers.

I knew the verses. I knew the promises. But *knowing* something is true and *feeling* it are not the same thing when grief has stripped you raw.

Still, God was patient.

He didn't demand faith I didn't have. He didn't wait for me to get my words right. He met me where I was—often in the quiet, sometimes through Scripture, sometimes through people, and once… in a way I never expected.

I share this next part prayerfully. What happened next was not a result of my faith—but a revelation of God's heart to me in a moment when mine was barely beating.

I don't know if the human imagination will ever be able to grasp the vastness of God's love. I so often doubted His nearness and underestimated His affection. The apostle Paul prayed that we might know—

> *... how wide, how long, how high, and how deep his love is. May you experience the love of Christ, though it is too great to understand fully. Then you will be made complete with all the fullness of life and power that comes from God.*
> *Ephesians 3:18-19 (NLT)*

Would that ever be possible? I was certain I had captured a glimpse of God's deep love two days earlier at the park. Like Ishmael, I pictured Jesus listening to my own heartbreak under the tree, my soul revived with living water from His deep well of grace.

I stepped into Mother's Day with an unexplainable sense of anticipation. I knew I could navigate the morning in God's strength. Gary and I led worship, every lyric a shield, deflecting the grief and emptiness that threatened my joy. As we stepped from the platform with tear-streaked faces, Zola, our elderly organist, slipped me a note: *"Please see me after the service."* I assumed it was about the music—maybe the volume.

When moms were invited to the platform, I joined my friends. Accepting the pink carnation became my way of affirming Karissa's life and my brief, irreplaceable role as her mother—a privilege, even on this painful path.

What happened next was not something I sought, nor something I would ever try to recreate. It was a gift—undeserved and unrepeated. And I know this with deep awareness: many faithful prayers do not end in moments like this. God's nearness is no less real when He remains silent.

But in that moment, God met me.

Not to erase my grief.
Not to explain His ways.
But to reassure me of one thing I desperately needed to know:

I had not been forgotten.

The certainty that wrapped around me that day didn't remove the ache of loss—but it anchored me inside it. I was still a mother who grieved. Still a woman learning how to breathe again. But I was no longer alone in the question of whether God had turned away.

He hadn't.

After the service, Zola approached me. I had no idea this encounter would become a pivotal hinge, swinging open a door that would forever alter my spiritual journey. She spoke with compassion and quiet authority:

"During worship, God gave me an incredible vision—of heaven. It wasn't for the church. Patty, I believe it was simply for you. I trust this will not deepen your pain. I only desire to be responsive to God."

Silence followed. I leaned in. Zola had stewarded God's spiritual gifts faithfully for decades, always encouraging the body of Christ with a prophetic word or vision (see Joel 2:28-32, Acts 2:16-17). I trusted this word would build, not break me.

Finally, as if waiting for a green light, Zola continued. *"In the vision, I saw Jesus surrounded by a sea of people. Closest to Him were the children. The atmosphere reverberated with celebration and dancing. Then He bent down, lifting a child into His arms. As He turned, I recognized the child—Karissa. He carried her the whole time you worshipped.* (Long pause) *He was telling her how much you love her, Patty. (*Another pause.) *He did one more thing: He gave her a kiss on the lips and whispered, "That one is from your mommy!"*

Tears rolled down my cheeks like water overflowing Niagara Falls. Completely swept up in God's love, I collapsed face-down on the carpet. This God-sized miracle was beyond comprehension. No one—not even Gary—had ever read my journal. Every doubt was removed: God saw me under the oak tree. He gathered my tears and searched out their contents. He waded through the tangle of uncertain prayers recorded within the pages of my journal.

In that moment, His voice was so clear to my soul:

I didn't ignore you or fail you when you begged me to raise Karissa. I have given her life—beyond your comprehension. The Spirit who raised Me (Jesus) from death to life, raised Karissa into unimaginable life. (See Romans 8:11)

You have known me as your Healer. I Am. However, I am so much more: "I am the Resurrection and the Life. The one who believes in

Me will live, even though they die." (John 11:25 NIV) You trusted her life would glorify me. It has—and it will.

Covenant promises I had forgotten, now erupted like fresh springs in my soul. They pumped life throughout my entire being:

My ways are higher than your ways. My thoughts higher than your thoughts. (See Isaiah 55:9) *I am not a man, who lies or changes his mind. I have never spoken and failed to act. I have never promised and not carried it through.* (See Numbers 23:19) *You can anchor your last thread of hope to My promises. I will fulfill each one—in My appointed time.*

I share this account, knowing some would rather dismiss it or explain it away than imagine a crazy-sounding miracle of this nature. I understand that impulse. I have never sought out oak-tree conversations or prophetic confirmations. Scripture never encourages us to build our faith on experiences. A sound faith is built on the timeless foundation of God's eternal Word. That has been my practice—day after day, decade after decade.

However, as I reflect on Scripture, I recognize how often it records jaw-dropping accounts of God's creative and *supernatural* involvement in the ordinary lives of men and women—not always changing outcomes in the way they hoped—but always present within them.

History is etched by a God who simply cannot stay away from His creation. Take, for example, the Gregorian calendar, used worldwide. It divides time into two distinct periods—Before Christ (BC) and Anno Domini (AD)—Latin for "in the year of our Lord." The very centerpiece of worldwide history is God stooping low in love, entering our world as a baby, born to a virgin. From Genesis to Revelation, He continually reveals Himself in both unexplainable and unrepeated ways.

One man heard God's voice echo from a burning bush (Exodus 3:1-17). Another walked with a limp after wrestling through the night with Him (Genesis 32:22-32). Only one child was rescued from a basket in the Nile (Exodus 2:3). Only one prophet saw fiery chariots circling an army that circled around him (2 Kings 6:14-18). Only one reluctant messenger survived a three-day taxi ride in the belly of a fish (Jonah 1-2). These occurrences don't seem to have reoccurrences. Perhaps our tendency would be to seek the experience more than we seek Him.

That realization didn't unsettle me. It amazed me. It seems God wasn't asking me—or you—to chase someone else's encounter. He wasn't prescribing repetition. He was inviting trust in His involvement.

On this unsuspecting Mother's Day, God Almighty pursued a heart too broken to be bold, too feeble to muster faith. By the Holy Spirit's power, His timeless promises pressed deeper into the softened clay of my soul.

My experience under the oak tree would never replace Scripture, but it served to confirm God's promise to us: *When you call, the Lord will answer. When you cry for help, He will say, 'Here I am.'* (See Isaiah 58:9).

God didn't meet me in this way because I prayed the right prayer or believed without wavering hope. *He met me because I was broken—and because He is the God who sees and cares.*

I want to invite you to consider your own story. Perhaps your own prayers remain unanswered. I pray Jesus could use my story to fill you with hope and strengthen you amid your pain.

If you've cried out and the sky felt silent, if you waited and nothing changed. I want to say this gently: God's nearness is not proven by the kind of answer we receive. I do not believe He comes to some but not to others, or loves one story more than another. The same God who revealed Himself to me—has not withdrawn Himself from you.

The Place of Promise is not about certainty or clarity—it's not about *how* God answers.

It's about *who* He is—a God who remains attentive, even when we are unsure—a God who sees, who hears the cries of His children, and who stays.

Your story is still unfolding. Keep seeking. Keep reaching.

You are not alone.

CHAPTER 23

UNEXPECTED JOY

"I have loved you, my people, with an everlasting love.
With unfailing love I have drawn you to myself.
Jeremiah 31:3 (NLT)

I will never possess the capacity to fully fathom the greatness of God—and I'm grateful for that. A God small enough to be completely understood would not be big enough to be trusted. His nature holds boundless mystery, stirring me to seek Him more.

At times, I catch glimpses of His grandeur—like when I stop to notice the ever-changing sunset and a starlit night. It's then that I find myself caught up in the words of the psalmist:

"The LORD merely spoke, and the heavens were created.
He breathed the word, and all the stars were born."
Psalm 33:6 (NLT)

I'm amazed that He continues to breathe over His creation. I find myself captivated by Scripture's accounts of His power—how He stopped the sun in its tracks and split seas wide open. Trying to imagine these wonders leaves me breathless.

Yet, what has undone me most has less to do with His power and more to do with His tenderness.

In the weeks following Mother's Day I found myself returning, again and again, to this holy mystery: Almighty God is not only vast enough to command the cosmos, but also willing to become small enough to enter the hidden places of private pain—and remain there with us. The Creator-God didn't rush past my raw sorrow. He didn't explain it away. He drew near. He wept with me. He stayed.

I am undone by the thought of God making Himself small—small enough to draw near to a broken girl under a tree. Near enough to collect her tears and record each one. Near enough to linger over the damp prayers in her journal. Near enough to interpret even whispered prayers too faint to become words.

I'm convinced God has always delighted in revealing Himself this way—not only through His vast creation, but through His closeness. Through His intimate presence. Through love that refuses to abandon us.

The prophet Zephaniah seemed to believe so:

For the Lord your God is living among you.
He is a mighty savior.
He will take delight in you with gladness.
With his love, he will calm all your fears.
He will rejoice over you with joyful songs."
Zephaniah 3:17 (NIV)

And here is what astonished me most: God's promises held—even when my faith faltered. He didn't withdraw. Instead, He turned up the volume on His love—not through magnificent wonders, but through the ordinary obedience of one of His servants: an elderly woman, unaware she was carrying the answer to trembling prayers—inked on journal pages and etched on God's heart.

I long for the day when I rest fully in Jesus' promises without hesitation. I suspect I'm not alone. Perhaps your trust has been tested too. Perhaps you wrestle somewhere between conviction and circumstances that seem to contradict it. For me, God used another person's willingness to listen and respond to His nudge. She gave Jesus room to step into a fragile space in my soul—where doubt had learned to hide.

When God Surprises

"Praise be to the Lord.
Not one word has failed of all the good promises
he gave through his servant Moses."
1 Kings 8:56 (NIV)

Over time, many of God's promises became anchors, offering comfort, hope, and even joy—though learning to fully trust them came with fits and starts.

Scripture holds thousands of promises. Friedrich Wilhelm Krummacher, a mid-nineteenth century preacher, once said, *"God's promises are, virtually, obligations that He imposes upon himself."*[xxxiii]

If that was true, then anchoring my hope there—however tentatively—felt like the safest place I could stand.

Ephesians 3:20 became one of my favorite anchors:

Now to him who is able to do immeasurably more
than all we ask or imagine,
according to his power that is at work within us...
Ephesians 3:20 (NLT)

More than we can imagine...

I'm hard-wired with a pretty strong imagination, so this verse stops me every time. It describes a God who not only answers, but often surprises—not always by changing outcomes, but by revealing His goodness in ways we never thought to ask for.

I have always loved surprises—and planning them, too.

Once, my enthusiasm nearly landed me in jail while orchestrating a birthday surprise for Gary. Everything unfolded without a wrinkle until I attempted to relocate his car from the diner where he was enjoying lunch with a friend. Gary looked up just in time to witness his car being 'stolen' from the parking lot. Assuming the worst, he called 911n and to this day I love that he thought someone would want to steal that rusty old Mustang.

What began as a joyful scheme—to whisk Gary away on a bike tour of the San Juan Islands—ended with flashing lights, a very unimpressed police officer, and an escorted drive back to the diner.

In the end, the surprise succeeded. The arrest did not.

Looking back, I smile at the escalating thrill of it—but I also wonder if our delight in surprising those we love offers a glimpse of God's heart toward us. Not because He always surprises us with answers we hope for, but because He delights in being attentive and near—even when our prayers remain unanswered.

Jesus assures us:

"If you, then, though you are evil,
know how to give good gifts to your children
[or your husbands]
how much more will your Father in heaven give good gifts
to those who ask him!"
Matthew 7:11 (NIV – emphasis mine)

That Mother's Day, I imagine God elbowing an angel and, eager to reveal a remarkable surprise, whispered, "*You think that caught Patty off-guard? Just wait... I'm not finished.*"

While my tears soaked the carpet, an astonishing and sacred gift was developing quietly in my womb. A tiny heart was beating to the rhythm of God's love—the thrum of another miracle.

Exactly one year after our deepest sorrow—the day an ambulance carried Karissa from our home—we crossed that same threshold again, this time carrying our second daughter, Hannah Joy. Her name means *full of grace*. And that is what she was—not a solution, not a replacement, but grace. Undeserved. An indescribable gift.

That Mother's Day moment didn't erase our grief. It did not answer every lingering ache or resolve the questions that still lived with us. But it became a marker—a quiet testimony that God was present in a season I once believed could only hold loss.

God arranges demonstrations of love amid the ruins of our circumstances. He suffers in our suffering and rejoices in renewing our joy. He not only stoops low to collect our tears; He also stoops low to surprise us with gifts only He can give. I imagine His eyes twinkle with joy when ours mist over in awe.

That Mother's Day reshaped the way I understand God's nearness. It did not promise clarity for every moment ahead, but it assured me that none of them would be unattended.

I'm convinced our life on earth is too brief to comprehend the kaleidoscope of God's love for us, but Jesus daily invites us to notice its ever-changing prisms—and to listen for His quiet melodies of love. He is always working, always weaving, always stooping low enough to hear even the faintest cry within your soul.

The same God who heard Ishmael's whispered cry—the same God who met me in my own unguarded moment—is listening to you.

He hears you—crying in the barren wasteland of your suffering.

The One who saw Hagar's turmoil, sees you—searching for something to sustain your weary heart.

And even in the place where your hope feels spent, He draws near—not always to explain, but to remain and to remind: He is your Refuge.

He is Your *Place of Promise*.

CHAPTER 24

THE GREATEST GIFT

And I will ask the Father,
and He will give you another Advocate,
who will never leave you.
John 14:16 (NLT)

Power To Soar

A few years ago, while speaking at a women's conference in the coastal town of Florence, Oregon, I slipped away between sessions and wandered down to the beach. I needed space—to breathe, to quiet my thoughts, to let the weight of the stories I'd shared settle.

The fall sun was warm. The shoreline buzzed with life. Frisbees sailed between friends. Couples walked hand in hand. Children crouched near the water, pockets full of shells and stones tossed back into the surf.

Further down the shore, something unusual caught my attention. Dozens of people were spreading what looked like massive beach blankets across the sand. Curious, I moved closer. What I thought were blankets were actually enormous ocean kites—laid out carefully, each one attended by its pilot and waiting for the wind.

To picture the scene, you'll need to forget the flimsy grocery-store kites of childhood—the kind with two thin dowels, a scrap of vinyl, a short tail, and a long string of hope.

I know, because I had one.

I remember running hard, straining for enough wind to carry it into the billowing clouds. The poor thing usually bumped along miserably behind me. On rare occasions, the breeze caught it and lifted it high above my head. If felt magical—pure joy—until it lost all sense of direction and lodged permanently in one of our old willow trees.

These beach kites were different. They were works of art—crafted to lift, designed to soar. Made of ripstop fabric and fiberglass frames, they were built to ride the powerful coastal winds.

I watched in wide-eyed wonder as the wind began to fill individual air-cells. Lifeless fabric trembled, took shape, and rose. Soon, the bright blue sky was alive with motion. Faces were turned upward, watching flying dragons and sea turtles, geometric forms and pirate ships dancing freely above the shore.

As I stood in quiet awe, one truth settled deeply in me: without the wind, even the most beautiful kite would remain lifeless. Their splendor depends entirely on a strong, unseen current and a skilled pilot. The wind lifted them from their dormant condition so they could rise, soar and dance to its rhythm.

So it is, with us.

Life has a way of deflating us. Loss, grief, and disappointment can leave us flattened by circumstances we never chose. And yet—even then—we remain held by a faithful Pilot. The same Spirit who raised Jesus from the dead fills the hollow places of our lives and teaches us how to rise again.

God knows life is simply too heavy to bear alone. From the beginning, He declared, *"It is not good for man to be alone"* (Genesis 2:18). That need—for communion, for presence—finds its fulfillment in Jesus.

Just before ascending to heaven, Jesus made a promise that must have sounded impossible to His disciples:

And be sure of this: I am with you always,
even to the end of the age."
Matthew 28:20b. (NLT)

How could He promise to remain—when He was leaving?

He explained it this way:

"And I will ask the Father,
and he will give you another Advocate,
who will never leave you."
John 14:16 (NLT)

Of all God's promises, this may be the greatest: the gift of His own Spirit—God's presence dwelling within us. Not distant. Not occasional. But near, faithful, and enduring—from beginning to end.

The word Jesus used is *Paraklētos*—often translated Advocate, Comforter, Helper, or Counselor. No single English word captures its depth. At its heart, it means *One who comes alongside.*

The Holy Spirit walks with us.

He defends when we are weary.

He comforts when grief overwhelms.

He helps when strength runs out.

He guides when the path feels unclear.

He is not a force we summon, but a Companion who stays—present in the sacred and the ordinary, in the magnificent and the mundane mess of life.

Around in Circles

I love those seasons when the wind feels strong—when joy rises easily, and God's nearness feels unmistakable. And there are other seasons when the air goes still, and all we can do is wait. I've known both.

After Karissa's death, I longed for the Spirit's breath to fill my life again. Instead, grief often left me running like that little girl with her grocery-store kite—straining, searching, exhausted—dashed hopes bouncing and bumbling behind.

At my doctor's suggestion, I joined a support group for parents who had also lost a child to SIDS. We sat in a circle of shared grief. They spoke of coping strategies, memorial rituals, and yearly traditions to keep their children's memories alive.

When it was my turn to speak, I looked around the circle—grateful for others who understood this painful journey. I could relate with the emotions shared and hoped it was safe enough to share mine.

Reluctantly, I began. "*I don't ever want to forget Karissa—I pray daily that I never will. But I didn't come here tonight to learn how to keep her memory alive. I came because I'm trying to keep myself alive.*"

The celebrations and activities they described—as tender and meaningful as they were—felt insufficient to reach the place where my own soul was bleeding. I looked around the circle at weary faces, fingers twisting tear-soaked tissues. I felt like I could cut the grief with a knife. Some had been walking this road for over a decade. I wondered how they were still standing.

Something stirred within me—not judgment, but compassion. A deep ache. I sensed that the life we were all longing for wasn't something any of us could manufacture or preserve on our own. So, with a trembling voice, I continued, "Jesus once told His disciples,

'The Spirit is the one who gives life. The flesh doesn't help at all' (John 6:63). I'm learning—slowly—that He is the only One who can reach wounds like these."

The facilitator interrupted gently, *"Thank you for sharing, sweetie. We try to keep this group a safe place for everyone, so we don't allow religion in our sessions."*

I nodded, understanding her concern. I didn't want to argue or disrupt the space. Still, the empty Kleenex boxes scattered around the circle testified to the emptiness I felt pressing in. *"I understand,"* I said quietly. *"I'm not interested in religion either. May I speak simply about my relationship with Jesus—the One who gives life? I know He wants to revive all our broken hearts."*

She smiled kindly and moved on. *"Stan, what highs and lows have you experienced this week?"*

I left that meeting with a heavy heart—not frustrated but grieved. I carried the faces of those parents with me, each one still bearing sorrow too large for words. I prayed they would encounter Life Himself in whatever way He chose to meet them.

I'm grateful for good ideas, meaningful practices, and for spaces where community is strengthened through shared experience. They matter. But I've come to believe that when grief drains us of breath, we need more than shared strategies—we need the Holy Spirit's sustaining presence. From the very beginning, Scripture tells us we were formed from the dust of the earth—beautifully shaped, yet lifeless—until God breathed His Spirit into us. His breath has always been what animates us, sustains us, and gives us fullness of life.

The Psalmist wrote:

"When you give them your breath, life is created."
Psalms 104:30a (NLT)

Beloved, you were never meant to carry life's weight alone—or to manufacture your own wind. The Spirit of God—the same breath that filled Adam's lungs and raised Christ from the dead—still moves through every barren place within us. Not to rush our healing. Not to force joy. But to stay. To steady us. To hold us when we no longer know how to hold ourselves. To lift us above what we cannot bear and restore what we thought was lost—hope.

Every promise in Scripture is carried on that same holy wind of His Spirit—steady, faithful, unseen, and strong enough to sustain you when your strength gives out.

He is the Greatest Gift.

So, Breathe.

Your life is held in Him—

The Place of Promise.

INVITING GOD TO BECOME YOUR PLACE OF PROMISE

Sometimes God arrives in our story like an unexpected gust of wind—filling us with hope beyond our circumstances. But other times, He finds us in our mess—and sits with us there.

In these chapters, we witnessed ways in which God met people in unexpected places: in abandonment, in despair, doubt, and in the emptiness of pain. Wherever you find yourself—He offers you, His companionship. He won't rush you onward through your grief or bypass the depths of your pain. He simply stays—and meets you where you are.

He invites you to linger with Him.

He doesn't expect tidy questions or strong faith. Come—exactly as you are.

Perhaps a picture from this chapter resonated with you. Maybe, you hope He hears your faint cry or sees you wandering without direction in the wilderness. Maybe you hope He meets you where you've fallen—alone in your grief. Or perhaps you need Him to come like a steady wind to fill your life with Himself.

God offers Himself—He offers His Promise—not as a swift answer to hurry you along in your grief, but to assure you He will never stop working within it:

You turned my wailing into dancing;
you removed my sackcloth and clothed me with joy.
Psalm 30:11–12b (BSB)

Though God's timing will rarely be your own, you can lean on His steadfast love and His faithfulness to His promises. Often, God is at work *while you wait*—steadying you to trust His heart even when His hand feels hidden.

The psalmist fought to remind Himself of God's faithfulness when surrounded with troubles:

"...I praise your name for your unfailing love and faithfulness;
for your promises are backed by all the honor of your name.
The Lord will work out his plans for my life—
for your faithful love, O Lord, endures forever."
Psalm 138:2,8a (NLT)

Over time, I pray you begin to see where His promises and your story converge. But for now, He offers His own strength while you stand on faith alone.

When you're ready, take a few quiet moments to reflect:

- Is there a specific promise that has sustained you in this season? Perhaps a promise from this section seemed to jump off the page into your spirit.
- Can you trace even a small thread of His faithfulness weaving itself into your story?

You may want to simply sit with the questions, talk to God about them or record your feelings in a journal. There is no right or wrong way to do this.

If it feels meaningful, write out the promise on a small card and save it somewhere you'll see it again. You don't have to strain hard to believe. You can simply receive a gentle promise by faith and return to it when your faith feels frail or your hope thin. Consider journaling what comes to mind at times when you revisit that promise.

Talk Honestly to God About Your Deepest Longings:

Some of our deepest prayers are the ones we whisper only to God. They feel too tender, too risky, or too personal to share anywhere else.

I prayed for months for a child. Many thought it would be too painful for me to have another girl—so, they prayed for a boy; one I couldn't compare to Karissa. I thanked them for their prayers, but in my secret place with God, I would whisper, *"God, I loved raising a girl. I wasn't finished with bows and bonnets."*

I wrote that longing in my journal. When our daughter, Hannah, was born, I connected the answer to those hidden prayers. God had been listening all along and changed my mourning into dancing.

"God weeps with us so that we may one day laugh with him," Jurgen Moltmann

If you are able Use the space below to name your own longings—especially the ones you've kept hidden. They are safe with Him. He receives them, understanding you fully. How might your longings be shaping a deeper trust in God—even now?

A PRAYER FOR A LONGING HEART:

Father,
You have heard my sighs.
You have seen my tears.
You know my deepest longings.
I offer them to You now.
Remind me that nothing escapes Your notice,
No promise escapes Your fulfillment.
Open my eyes to the quiet ways

You are already at work—
Redeeming my story.
You have met me before.
Please, meet me again—
In Your way.
In Your Time.
Awaken my heart to see Your goodness.
Weave it through the circumstances of my story.
Tune my ears to hear Your voice.
My heart to Your faithfulness.
I love you, Lord—
My strength, My hope. My source.
My Place of Promise.
Amen.

SECTION NINE

The Place of Power

For All My Weakness

"Yes, my soul, find rest in God;
my hope comes from him."

Psalm 62:5 NIV

CHAPTER 25

BOUND TO GRACE

So do not fear, for I am with you;
do not be dismayed, for I am your God.
I will strengthen you and help you;
I will uphold you with my righteous right hand.
For I am the LORD, your God,
who takes hold of your right hand and says to you,
Do not fear; I will help you.
Isaiah 41:10,13 (NIV)

Rooted

In the months after Karissa's death, I learned that grief not only shattered my heart—it threatened to loosen my roots in Christ. It became increasingly easy to *look* alive while quietly dying inside. People nudged me to move on, to distract myself with other things, but I couldn't keep pace. They expected rejoicing, not grieving. After all, I was pregnant again. It was a miracle. And Karissa had already been gone seven months.

I thought I was doing a good job hiding my pain—until one day, during a baby dedication, memories surfaced and tears spilled out without warning. As I stood there, one friend, cradling her infant, whispered sharply, *"You've got to get over this, Patty. It's time to move on."* She may have meant well, and she may have even been right. But I didn't know *how* to do that without losing myself in the process.

I tried to keep going—to do what was expected, to appear strong—but the harder I worked at holding it together, the more I sensed the real danger: I wasn't just tired or overwhelmed. I was at risk of living *apart* from God rather than remaining *rooted* in Him. What I needed wasn't another strategy for surviving loss; I needed to stay firmly attached to the Source of life—and I needed help to do that.

It seems humanity has had a long history of trying to attain life outside the One who gives it. The serpent deceived Adam and Eve into believing God was withholding something good from them. They imagined freedom but found failure. Instead of life, they felt loss. They reached for autonomy, but ended up alienated—from God, from one another, and even from themselves. Disconnected from the Source of Life, they began to die—like a tree severed from its roots.

That image felt painfully familiar to me.

One of our family's most cherished Christmas traditions had always been the annual hunt for our tree. The attachment ran deep, tracing all the way back to my childhood. It didn't matter whether we tramped through the woods, wandered through a tree farm, or pulled into a hardware store lot—choosing the *right* tree was important business. I felt the personal responsibility of selecting the right one.

Dad would carry it inside, anchor it in a basin of water, and by evening, the room was transformed: the fragrance, the glow of lights on the fresh branches, the sparkle of the ornaments—it all signaled that Christmas had arrived.

Gary and I carried that tradition into our own family, celebrating it with enough enthusiasm and festivities to justify a national holiday. Though I still loved the adventure of searching through the woods, a local tree farm often served to keep up the tradition. Each year, Gary gently suggested that a pre-lit, artificial tree could save time, money, and effort. Yet year after year, he graciously welcomed a real one into our home.

I greeted its arrival with nostalgic carols and a generous supply of sugar water, hoping to prolong its stay. That first day, the tree drank deeply—like a traveler needing refreshment after crossing the desert.

For a couple of weeks, the tree was glorious.

And then, almost imperceptibly, something shifted.

It no longer had the strength to sip even a small bit of water. The fragrance faded. The needles grew brittle—the branches bare. Soon after New Year's, we would reluctantly drag it outside and prop it among the wintering plants—as if the cold air might somehow invigorate it for a few more days. I refused to admit the futility of all my efforts to keep the tree 'alive'.

The truth was unavoidable: the moment we severed it from its roots; it was already dead.

I could decorate it. I could offer its mortal wound a few sips of sweetened water. I could enjoy its fleeting beauty, but it swiftly surrendered all pretense. Nothing I did could restore the life it once had.

That realization lingered with me—because our souls are not much different.

Without a living connection to God, we are a tree severed from its roots—we may appear vibrant for a season: We might find ways to cope. We may attend support groups. We may try strategies that dull grief's sharp edges. We may hope that time alone will soften the ache. And sometimes, it works—for a while.

But separated from The Source of Life, our best efforts only offer a cheap imitation of the life Jesus longs to give us.

Jesus once said it this way:

"I am the true vine... Remain in me, and I will remain in you. For a branch cannot produce fruit if it is severed from the vine... Apart from me you can do nothing" (John 15:1–5 NLT).

I don't hear those words as a rebuke. I hear them as an invitation—Jesus was clarifying reality. True vitality doesn't come from self-effort or sentiment—it flows from union with Him. Our brittle souls are regenerated when they're rooted to the Source of life.

And here is where grace meets us: God doesn't discard what is broken. He restores it. His Spirit reaches into what feels dry and dying and begins to renew our life from His own endless supply. He doesn't grow weary of reviving us. He offers Himself freely—until even ordinary soil becomes holy ground.

Super Sweet Lessons

I don't claim to be much of a gardener, but I do love planting things and watching them grow. Any real success I've had is thanks to friends and experts who were generous enough to share what they knew.

One of my favorite plants is a cherry tomato called the *Super Sweet 100*. The fruit tastes like candy. One year, every nursery in town sold out of them. Still, I optimistically held a space in my garden—just in case. By mid-June, it was clear I'd missed my window.

Around that same time, Gary was sweating through the summer heat while laying a backyard patio. Needing a break, he suggested a quick stop at a nearby nursery to see if they had any leftover plants. The gardener chuckled at our optimism but agreed to check "behind the barn" where they kept a few unsold plants.

Moments later, he emerged smiling ear to ear, holding the last surviving Super Sweet 100. A mid-summer Christmas miracle—mine for under a dollar.

Eager not to waste this treasured gift, I planted it immediately. Recalling a technique from a gardening podcast, I dug a horizontal trench instead of a deep hole, hoping to warm more of the root system and increase the yield.

It made perfect sense—until I tried to bend the mature stalk upright.

Snap.

Half the plant remained in my hand. The other half lay buried beneath the soil. I stood frozen, wondering how I would explain that I had just ended the life of the last Super Sweet in the Inland Northwest.

Panic has a way of fueling creativity.

I slipped past Gary, grabbed a roll of packing tape from the kitchen, and returned to the garden. I dug up the lower portion, carefully aligned the broken stem, and bound the two together. Abandoning the trench idea, I buried the plant deep enough to hide the tape.

When Gary ventured to the garden in a few days, he could bear the bad news: *Patty, I hate to tell you this. Your Super Sweet didn't make it.*

I rehearsed my response: *NO! Are you kidding me? It looked so healthy.*

Days passed, and to my surprise, 'Super' wasn't dead at all—it was thriving. Tiny yellow blossoms covered its branches. When I finally confessed the story to Gary, we laughed in amazement and enjoyed watching that patched-up plant produce more fruit than any tomato plant we'd ever grown.

I don't share this story because it holds a clever gardening hack. I share it because I recognized myself in that plant after Karissa's death.

Suffering has a way of snapping us at the stem. And if we try to survive apart from Jesus—the true Vine—life gradually drains away. Without His strength flowing into us, all vision of life, fullness, and fruitfulness is over.

But when we reach for Him, desperately and imperfectly, He binds us to Himself.

Jesus used the word *remain* eleven times in John 15 alone. The Greek word *meno* can mean abide, dwell, remain. My favorite translation is ***Stay**—here.*

Through joy and sorrow, strength and weakness, through your best days and worst days—and every day in between, Jesus is saying, "*I will stay with you. Will you stay with me?*"

Tragedy may threaten to sever us, but God—the Master Gardener—does not abandon what is broken. He grafts us back to Himself. And when life flows again, it doesn't erase the wound—it redeems it, producing beauty and fruitfulness instead of the twisting pinch of sorrow. He offers life, despite a painful past.

Jesus went to the cross not only to forgive sin but to end the separation it caused. Our disobedience cut us off, but He reconnected us on the cross. When we say, *"Jesus, I give You my life,"* He offers us His—binding our weakness to His strength and causing hope to flow into stories we thought were finished.

This means that anyone who belongs to Christ
has become a new person.
The old life is gone; a new life has begun!
2 Corinthians 5:17 (NLT)

Chapter 26

ALIVE... AGAIN

By the word of the LORD *the heavens were made,*
and by the breath of His mouth all their host.
Let all the earth fear the LORD*;*
let all the inhabitants of the world stand in awe of him!
For he spoke, and it came to be;
he commanded, and it stood firm.
Psalm 33:6, 8-9 (ESV)

Like a skilled gardener grafting a broken stem back to the vine, God reconnected my life to His. Once rejoined to Him, He does more than hold us together—He breathes life into us. The same Spirit who rooted us in Christ empowers us to flourish again.

As I invited His presence into my life day after day—sometimes weakly, sometimes desperately—He began restoring strength I didn't know I still possessed. I became more comfortable spending time alone at home. I planted a garden and shared the space with neighbors who liked to garden. I started to meet with a group of women to read and pray together. They motivated me to open my Bible more. Their surrounding presence renewed hope I thought grief had buried—and performance had severed. What once felt like an emotional graveyard slowly began to stir.

Scripture never hides the devastating effects of a life separated from God. The book of Judges traces the unraveling of a people who chose what was right in their own eyes. The result was spiritual chaos.

And yet—even then—God never stopped reaching to restore them. He pursued.

Centuries after the era of Israel's judges, when they believed themselves beyond repair, God gave the prophet Ezekiel a vision. (See Ezekiel 37) He led him into a valley littered with dry bones—a landscape of utter desolation. God asks him a startling question:

"Son of man, can these bones live?"

If He had asked me that question in my own valley, I might have rushed to a practical answer. But Ezekiel wasn't so quick to limit The Author of Life.

"Sovereign Lord, You alone know."

When God enters the equation, possibility shifts. *"I am the Lord, the God of all mankind. Is anything too hard for me?" (Jeremiah 32:27 NIV)*

Then, God gave Ezekiel what must have sounded like an impossible assignment: *"Speak a prophetic message to these bones and say, 'Dry bones, listen to the word of the Lord! I am going to put breath into you and make you live again... Then you will know that I am the Lord."*

I couldn't read this passage without recognizing myself there. A valley of brittle bones—a fitting description of a soul gouged by pain: stripped bare, scattered, and hollowed by loss—destruction across a landscape of what should have been a fertile valley.

And yet God spoke into this graveyard. Could He do it again? In me? In us?

"Your story isn't over. Listen to the Word of the Lord."

Perhaps you ache to hear these words, too.

Doctors may say, "*There's nothing more we can do*".

A supervisor may whisper, *"Your position is being eliminated."*

A spouse may announce, *"We're finished. I'm done trying."*

But beneath every human report is another Voice beckoning: *Hear the Word of the Lord.*

As I read the account, Ezekiel reminded me, man is not in control. God is. Man's report doesn't determine our fate. God does. He has the final say. His Word carries authority over every valley.

Ezekiel spoke to the bones… and suddenly the valley trembled. Bones rattled, moving toward one another. Sinews knit. Flesh formed. Skin covered what was once scattered. Ezekiel was no longer surrounded by skeletons, but by hundreds of lifeless corpses—bodies without breath. I would have preferred the original pile of dry bones.

For Ezekiel's sake and ours, I'm glad corpse-valley wasn't the end of the vision. God wasn't finished working.

At God's instruction, Ezekiel called for the 'wind'—*ruach* in Hebrew: wind, breath, and Spirit. *Come from every direction. Breathe into these corpses so they may live.*

Ruach entered them. They rose to their feet. A vast army restored by the breath of God. "*These bones are my people."* God explained. *"They say, 'We are cut off from God.' But I will put my Spirit in you, and you will live." (See Ezekiel 37:11, 14)*

Those words resounded within me: *"You will live."*

I needed those words—repeatedly. Perhaps you feel the same way. Maybe the landscape of your life looks hopeless—beyond fixing. Yet I believe God still enters bleak valleys—and when He does, things simply begin to change.

"*I will put breath in you, and you will live."*

You can be certain of this: Where the Spirit of God is, there is life.

This promise doesn't spare us from suffering. It doesn't deny valleys. But it does assure us that separation is not our final state. When we feel like a kite with no breeze, a tree severed from its roots, like bones scattered in the desert—it's not the end of the story.

It wasn't the end for Ezekiel.

It wasn't the end for me.

And I trust it is not the end for you.

Open My Ears to Hear

Pain has a way of narrowing our vision and dulling our hearing. When my strength was weak and my hope waning, I became desperate for God's voice above the deafening noise of pain. I would often confess to God, *"This is what I feel; but, God, I need to hear what is true."*

I've never heard God speak audibly—but I have heard Him, again and again—through His Word. Encouraging. Directing. Revealing. Training. He knew I needed more than words on a page. I needed revelation. I needed Him to breathe over the words until they became alive inside me.

Scripture shows us that God speaks in many ways—through circumstances, people, dreams, and desires. Yet the primary way He reveals His heart is through His Word. Every other voice must bow to the Truth He has already spoken.

When I open Scripture now, I often begin with a simple request: *Holy Spirit, open my ears to Your voice. Open my heart to Your guidance. Let me see what You want to show me.*

When Ezekiel responded to God's voice, life followed. I've found the same rhythm to be helpful—listen, respond, and watch what God breathes into motion.

God makes staggering promises regarding the power of His Word: It revives the weary. It gives wisdom to the simple. It brings joy to the sorrowful. It illuminates dark paths. It warns, and it rewards. (See Psalm 19:7-11)

Beloved, you were formed by the affection of His heart and animated by the breath of His Spirit. And He now offers His Word as oxygen to your lungs—the sustaining life-source for wounded souls.

Scripture remains living and active because the Spirit of God still breathes over it.

Sometimes, I read a passage I've read a hundred times—and I see something altogether new: A dimension of His nature I hadn't noticed before. Timely instruction, previously hidden. Guidance for a dark valley. A promise I hadn't heard before. Like the turning of a kaleidoscope, the same pieces rearrange and reveal something profoundly wonderful.

I can't do anything besides marvel: *"God! I've never seen You like this before."*

All Scripture is God-breathed. It is not static. We are invited to inhale what God exhales over us. That alone changes how I approach it.

This God-breathed Book did what time, willpower, and human encouragement couldn't do for me. It was giving life where grief had drained it.

It was living water, reviving me (John 7:38).

It nourished me with satisfying milk when I was fragile (1 Peter 2:2-3).

It was bread for my starving soul (Matthew 4:4).

It opened my ears to hear God's voice (Psalm 119:18).

It loosened chains I didn't know I was still wearing (John 8:32).

The Psalms, in particular, became companions. The psalmist's prayers startled me with their raw honesty: songs of lament, praise, accusation, and wonder revealed hearts laid bare before God. The psalms gave me words when my voice felt vacant. It offered language for the longings I struggled to name.

Jesus prayed these psalms regularly. As I followed His example, it drew me deeper into communion with God. By reading the Psalms aloud, they've become something more than the prayerful songs of past believers. They expressed my own varied needs and desperate prayers.

I've come to see that I will only trust God to the extent I know His heart. And He hasn't hidden it from us. He revealed it fully in Christ. I began to see God through the Gospels in a way that captured my heart—Jesus' life, His joy, His compassion, His prayer, His rest, His miracles—even His suffering revealed the magnificent wonder of God's nature. Jesus said, *"If you've seen Me, you've seen the Father."* (See John 14:9)

And as I searched to know Him in Scripture, I began to find Him on every page. The Bible wasn't intended to be merely instruction. It is a revelation: a love story of a God who re-members our dismembered hearts—binding what was shattered back to Himself.

I learned to expect that, when I was still enough to listen, He would speak.[xxxiv]

And as I listened, slowly—almost imperceptibly at first, life started to return.

Jesus renewed me through His Word. The brittle leaves of my broken heart slowly began to unfurl. Hope moved again through veins I thought had collapsed for good. Small buds appeared where winter had settled in.

He was not erasing my story—He was restoring my soul within it. Karissa was still gone. Her laughter, absent from within our walls. That valley didn't disappear. But breath had entered it.

The Spirit who hovered over the chaos in Genesis, who revived Ezekiel's valley of dry bones, who raised Jesus from the grave—began filling the hollow places in me. It didn't happen all at once, but He was breathing over me—awakening me to life again.

I began to ask Him: "*God, what do You want to show me about Yourself? What do You want to shape in me? Where do You want to work through me?*"

There was no formula—no strength of my own—God was simply meeting me right where I was. Breathing. Speaking… life over me. As I allowed the tethering tape of Scripture to fasten my thoughts to His, old thinking patterns began to shift. The Spirit used His Word to rewire the way I saw our loss, my identity, and the future.

Perhaps you doubt your ability to hear God's voice. Invite Him into your valley. It's where He wants to be.

Avoid getting caught up in performance. Simply find a rhythm that fits your life. A quiet corner. A few minutes. An open heart… and then ask God to help.

Whether you choose a psalm, a Gospel passage, or a reading plan—expect an encounter. In the words of Martyr Dietrich Bonhoeffer, *"When you read the Bible, you must think that here and now God is speaking to me."*[xxxv]

You may discover what ancient Job found to be true:

I have treasured the words of His mouth
more than my daily bread.
Job 23:12b (NIV)

He still revives.

He still empowers.

Jesus said He came that we might have life—abundant life. Not without valleys or without scars—But Spirit-breathed.

Life.

Picture your Master Gardener bending over the fractured places of your story, whispering into your doubt, "*This is not the end. I am here. Let My power restore you. Let My Word renew you.*"

Breathe. Simply Breathe.

CHAPTER 27

STRONGER THAN YOU KNOW

O my Strength, I will sing praises to you,
for you, O God, are my fortress,
the God who shows me steadfast love.
Psalm 59:17 (ESV)

Working out in a public fitness center is humbling. I've found myself on a mat beside someone effortlessly completing forty, perfectly executed, full-body push-ups, while I wobble through twelve—on my knees. Meanwhile, someone nearby presses forty-five pounds overhead while I debate whether ten might be overly ambitious.

Strength has come slowly for me—incrementally—through consistency that rarely felt impressive. But over time, ten push-ups became twenty. Weights increased. Muscles strengthened. The out-of-reach became attainable.

I wonder if the body is a living parable for the soul. Spiritual strength grows the same way—through small, faithful turns toward God when everything in us feels weak.

One morning while reading the Psalms, this one felt written for me:

Blessed are those whose strength is in you,
whose hearts are set on pilgrimage.
As they pass through the Valley of Baka,
they make it a place of springs;
the autumn rains also cover it with pools.

They go from strength to strength,
till each appears before God in Zion.
Psalm 84:5-7 NIV

The Valley of Baka. I knew that valley well. It is often translated the *"Valley of Weeping*."

In the months after Karissa's death, I was keenly aware of my spiritual deficiency… yet a greater Source was quietly at work within me. The psalmist recognized a strength beyond himself, offered to those who accept Jesus' invitation to remain in Him. His is a strength that doesn't fail even when our own resources run dry. It seems those who move forward are the ones who know they can't tackle the pain-scarred journey alone.

This passage included a line that puzzled me: *"They make it a place of springs*."

Wait—*they* make it? That sounded a lot like self-sufficiency to me. But here's the truth: God doesn't *make* it a place of springs. He *is* The Spring, giving refreshment to those who dig, strength to those who seek—living water to quench our bone-weary souls.

Let us… press on to know him…
he will come to us like the winter rains,
like the spring rains that water the earth."
Hosea 6:3 (NIV)

God invites us to put His power to the test—to lean fully on His strength—and discover it holds. He steadies, comforts, and celebrates each small, determined step we take toward Him. Your progress may feel insignificant, but God honors every intention to seek Him on life's steepest climbs. With each step, He increases both our endurance and our desire to keep going.

You may know someone who seemed to navigate suffering with confidence and strength. Maybe, as you watched them emerge from a painful season into joy and peace, you wonder what's wrong with your soul. The journey through suffering is not a foot-race. You are not behind. Like you, they gained that ground one small, steady step after another. Allow their journey to remind you that progress is possible… and every step is producing something new—even when we can't see it happening.

God's Surgeon Table

The summer following Karissa's death, I sat across from a spiritual mentor, frustrated and exhausted by my inability to "move on" within the timelines others thought reasonable. I felt behind—in healing, in joy, in faith. With deep compassion, He challenged me:

You can try to hurry the process along, try to peel the wound back before it's healed, but you'll simply end up with a festering, disabling wound. You'll spend the rest of your days trying to hide a gnarly, twisted scar.

Or, you can rest on God's surgeon's table and allow His skilled hands to gently clean out the infection, the stench, the torn tissue, and to stitch your heart with sutures that will one day form a delicate scar from which to share your story.

I longed for the patience to heal. I understood I would do lasting damage if I tried pushing harder and further than my faith was ready for. I wanted to allow God's deeper work—His complete healing. But to be honest, the slow nature of it all made me uncomfortable and embarrassed.

There's no fast track through suffering—the book of Job proves this. It's a long story—forty-two chapters of agonizing, unchanging misery. An arduous road of grey—just pain and heartache, one chapter after chapter. When suffering lingers, it makes those around us uncomfortable—they simply need it to end. Yet pain defies the easy fix. It doesn't respond to *snap-out-of-it* remedies.

Fellow pilgrims through Baka understand this slow pilgrimage. So—I sought out faith-filled friends who had walked the path before me. I listened. I learned, and I borrowed their courage. They steadied my faith when my knees buckled, and I wanted to give up. They cheered me on—one step at a time.

Strong and Courageous

Strength grows so slowly; we don't always recognize it taking place within us. Yet every step of faith prepares us for moments and possibilities yet to be revealed. The Bible records a vivid picture of what this looked like for God's people—and what it required of them.

Joshua led God's people into a promise they doubted would ever materialize. Forty years earlier, God delivered them from Egypt, promising to give them a land of their own. He sustained them with manna at dawn, water from rocks, quail from the sky, and shoes that refused to wear out.

But the Israelites grew disillusioned by God's unhurried timing. They weren't willing to worship Him in the liminal space—that no-man's land between the giving and arrival of His promise. God was looking for a people who would worship along the way—those who would seek His goodness within the struggle and trust His heart when the wilderness grew long.

Though I didn't want to be among the desert complainers, I often found myself there. When God's timing stretched longer than expected—when the road was harder and the pace slower than I imagined—I joined the disgruntled. And when I quit trusting in His power—I lost vision of the promises He had whispered to my soul.

Now Joshua was standing with a new generation and another barrier—between them and the promised land: the Jordan River at flood stage. The message was unmistakable: They would never outgrow their need of God's intervening power on their journey.

God told Joshua:

Be strong and courageous.
Do not be afraid or discouraged.
The Lord your God is with you wherever you go.
Joshua 1:9 (CSB)

God wasn't asking Joshua to manufacture bravery or muster pseudo-strength for his calling. He was inviting him to lean his full weight on God's divine strength. God was promising to be *Their Place of Power—never leaving, never forsaking them.*

When I read those words in my own valley, they felt less like a command and more like a promise.

It seems our power to walk out our hard stories, only gains strength as we trust God's involvement within them.

Do you feel impatient with God's timing? Are you discouraged or weary? If so, I am praying you will hear His Spirit whisper encouragement into your soul:

Be strong—for I am your strength.
Be courageous—for I go before you.
Do not fear—for I am beside you.
Do not falter—for I uphold you.
Cling to My Word—and you will not fall.
Trust My heart—one day you will see My hand.
Keep Watch—and you will witness My work.

The Master Canner

Years ago, I attempted to can apple butter. The apple butter was delicious. The sealing process? Catastrophic.

I had assembled baskets of warm bread and apple butter and delivered them to friends. I was overjoyed by their responses. I counted the whole project a win—until we shared dinner with one of those friends months later.

Our host carried warm rolls, and her saved jar of apple butter to the table. As she loosened the outer ring, the cap shot off like a rocket. We were baptized with fermented failure. Apparently, my preservation skills needed serious intervention.

God, however, is a master at preserving truth. The promises He seals on the pantry shelves of our hearts never spoil. They don't ferment. They never expire.

The prophet, Jeremiah, once wrote,

"When I discovered your words, I devoured them.
They are my joy and my heart's delight,
for I bear your name, O LORD God of Heaven's Armies."
Jeremiah 15:16 (NLT)

I'm amazed how verses I clung to twenty years ago still nourish me today. Truths stored in one season have strengthened another. The Holy Spirit does more than inspire Scripture—He preserves it within us and retrieves it at precisely the right moment.

When grief threatened to empty me, God reached for promises I had stored long before Karissa died. He opened them and revived me through them. As He fueled me with His enduring promises, strength returned. Not all at once—but enough to take another step toward healing.

Stronger Than You Know

You may feel weak. You may feel behind. You may feel like your faith is embarrassingly small. But if you are returning to Him—however haltingly—you are stronger than you know. For He is *The Place of Power.* He will give you strength for every step.

Sometimes that step may look like opening your Bible again, or whispering one honest prayer, or choosing not to let go when you feel so far behind.

You may not see muscle forming in your soul. But heaven does... and is rejoicing.

And one day, you will look back and realize: while you thought you were barely surviving, God was quietly building spiritual muscle for the road ahead.

Contrary to popular opinion, our strength was never meant to originate in us. It flows from God— our *Place of Power*.

INVITING GOD TO BECOME YOUR PLACE OF POWER

Beloved, we were never designed to generate power on our own. We were created to receive it—from the Vine who never withers, from the Breath who revives the driest bones, from the Word who steadies trembling hearts, from our loving Father who whispers courage into the places we feel weakest.

Power grows within us slowly, almost imperceptibly—one decision today, another tomorrow—the Spirit breathing life where hope has worn thin and Scripture growing roots in our souls.

This is how transformation grows—without instant results. We trust God to guide us from uncertainty to steadiness, from emptiness to renewal, from weakness to strength.

Jesuit priest, Pierre Teilhard de Chardin (1891-1955) once said, "*Above all, trust in the slow work of God.*"

As you enter this reflective space, I pray it becomes your meeting place with God—the place where His Spirit blows over every desolate valley. May you recognize ways His strength has held you, times His Word has nourished you, moments His breath has revived you. The fact you are at this spot in this book is a testament to God's power at work within you. You have made it so far–one step at a time. Congratulations!

When you feel ready, invite Him to meet you again… right here—right now—to lead you into the next step of your story—stronger than you can imagine, held by *The Place*, whose power will never fail.

God used the passages listed below to strengthen me in moments of profound weakness. I pray by His grace, He would breathe over them, causing them to come alive in you— strengthening your life with renewed courage. May they become flame to set your heart on fire.

So, I invite you to settle into a quiet place where you can be alone with God for a few minutes.

When you're ready, pick a verse to read, either silently or out loud. Ask The Spirit of Revelation to open your spirit to the work He wants to do in you. He welcomes you to lean in and lean on the power of His Word.

Your regulations remain true to this day,
for everything serves your plans.
If your instructions hadn't sustained me with joy,
I would have died in my misery.
Psalm 119:91-92

God is our refuge and strength,
a helper who is always found
in times of trouble.
Therefore, we will not be afraid,
though the earth trembles
and the mountains topple
into the depths of the seas,
though its waters roar and foam
and the mountains quake with its turmoil.
Psalm 46:1 HCSB

Do not fear, for I am with you;
do not be afraid, for I am your God.
I will strengthen you; I will help you;
I will hold on to you with my righteous right hand.
Isaiah 41:10 HCSB

Scripture I'm Meditating on from Section 9

Did a verse or passage stand out to you from this section? Take some time this week to focus on it. If it's helpful, record your initial thoughts in your favorite journal.

What I Sense God Saying

As you re-read the passage slowly, invite the Holy Spirit to speak. *What is God revealing—about Himself, about you, or about your situation?*

Where I need Strength

Name the place in your life that feels weak, weary, stretched, or vulnerable. *Where do you sense your strength running thin?*

A Step of Trust

God will strengthen you one step at a time. *What is one small act of obedience, surrender, or trust He is inviting you into?*

Declaring Truth Over My Heart

Turn the Scripture you are meditating on into a short prayer or declaration. *Example: "Lord, You are my refuge and strength. I will not fear."*

Evidence of His Faithfulness

Look back over the week. *Where did you sense God helping, sustaining, steadying, or guiding you?*

My Prayer Today

Pour out your heart to God. *Tell Him what you need.*

A PRAYER IN YOUR TIME OF WEAKNESS

Oh, Father of Power, Love and Mercy, I am overtaken by Your relentless pursuit of my crippled heart. I feel unworthy to dwell in

Your presence; but You have carried me to Yourself and offered me an everlasting place at Your table. You long to nourish me from the banquet of Your Word. I receive it, Lord.

Jesus, please reveal Yourself to me every time I draw near. Teach me Your ways. Please strengthen my soul with the breath of Your Spirit. Fill me. Steady me on my feet again. Guide me on Your pathways so that my life might produce fruit that brings You glory.

Holy Spirit, please carry me to The Place of Power–I have no strength of my own. Intertwine my frayed soul with the cords of Your boundless love. I rely on You. I center my life on You, My Vine, My Breath, My Life. You are My Place of Power, always willing to renew me in Your presence.

I am Yours.

SECTION TEN

The Place of Purpose
In All My Pain

I will sing of your strength; I will sing aloud
of your steadfast love in the morning.
For you have been to me a fortress
and a refuge in the day of my distress.

Psalm 59:16 ESV

CHAPTER 28

YOUR LIFE... GOD'S MASTERPIECE

He has given me a new song to sing,
a hymn of praise to our God.
Many will see what he has done and be amazed.
They will put their trust in God.
Psalm 40:3 (NLT)

Repaired

Several years ago, I was flying home from a writer's conference in central California. I had prayerfully pitched this book idea, hoping someone might help place this manuscript into the hands of individuals who could benefit from it.

Exhausted, I decided to rest my word-weary mind by thumbing through the in-flight magazine tucked into the seat-pocket in front of me. I felt like a five-year-old—ignoring the text and scanning the photos—until one image stopped me.

It was a photograph of a vase, fractured and asymmetrical, its cracks traced with veins of gold.

I dog-eared the page as my eyes involuntarily closed, but the image lingered. Curiosity soon eclipsed my need for a nap. I had to read the article.

It described an ancient Japanese art called Kintsugi—"*golden repair*." Broken vessels were not merely restored; their value increased in proportion to the gold used to mend them. The more shattered the original piece, the more valuable it became.

These pieces stood in stark contrast to my own attempts at repairing keepsakes with beads of glue. My repairs could disguise a flaw and spare a sentimental item from the trash, but the original beauty—and purpose—was always lost.

Kintsugi doesn't hide fractures. The artist highlights them.

Instead of concealing the break, gold fills the seams, transforming the damage into part of the beauty.

The article was a parable of my life—once terribly broken, now slowly restored by God's relentless grace. He never left me in suffering, and He never discarded what was shattered—He stayed with my broken heart.

So much of our energy is spent trying to disguise our limping souls. We posture our lives to conceal our past, hoping no one will trace the cracks back to our deepest pain. But hiding fractures often leads to isolation, insincerity, and shame. Feeling like impostors in our own skin, we hold relationships at arm's length.

I am grateful I lacked the strength to hide. My only option was to entrust the rubble of my heart to God.

Over the decades, He has patiently gathered every misshapen piece, finding value in every fragment—and fashioned my story into a vessel marked by His craftsmanship. He *re-membered* the pieces of my life with His presence.

He offers the same for anyone whose story feels beyond repair—binding brokenness with the golden repair of His faithful love.

"If you have a pulse, you still have a purpose,"[xxxvi] declares Katherine Wolf—who knows firsthand the pain of broken bodies, broken brains, and broken hearts. She also bears witness to God's redemptive nature at work in her own hard story.

If we understood the breadth of God's love, His wisdom and care, we would place our shattered stories into His hands without hesitation—and watch Him form a masterpiece only He can complete.

Repaired lives throughout history testify of a God who ascribes value to every soul. And when the broken hands of a busted world catch a glimpse of our mended stories, hope tilts their gaze toward a God who can do the impossible.

Perhaps even now your soul releases a whispered prayer: *God, can You make something beautiful from this?* And in the mystery of lifting them up to Him, something altogether lovely begins to form.

God redeems those places you allow Him to touch. And in time, you begin to see not only His power — but how personally you are loved.

The Apostle Paul describes it this way:

"Now the essence of this new life is no longer mine,
for the Anointed One lives his life through me
—we live in union as one.
My new life is empowered by the faith of the Son of God
who loves me so much that he gave himself for me,
dispensing his life into mine!"
Galatians 2:20b (TPT)

My life is no longer mine—it belongs to Him. I have learned the quiet contentment of being loved by God and offering myself to His purposes.

A terminally ill monk named Dominique Voillaume left a small monastery in Saint-Rémy to live out his terminal days among the people in a Paris slum. He wrote:

"If God wants it to, my life will be useful through my word and witness. If he wants it to, my life will bear fruit through my prayers

and sacrifices. But the usefulness of my life is his concern, not mine. It would be indecent of me to worry about that."[xxxvii]

God calls us his *masterpiece* (see Ephesians 2:10). The Greek word is *poēma*—you are God's poem. Every stanza of your life—even the dark lines of suffering—are woven into redemption.

If you are breathing—and I can safely assume you are—God is still writing your priceless poem.

The Refiner's Fire

Sometimes we hesitate to surrender our stories. We don't want certain chapters repaired. We want them erased. I've begged God to tear pages from my story, convinced nothing good could grow from the devastation. I know I'm not the only one who has felt this.

When Mount St. Helens erupted in 1980, its violent blast reduced the forested mountainside into a lunar landscape. Ash and rock, from miles below the earth's surface, covered everything. Many wondered if anything good would ever emerge from the massive piles of ash and rock.

Yet expert glass artisans discovered beauty hidden in the ruins. Under intense heat, volcanic ash transformed into luminous glass. Skilled glassblowers shaped it into rare, irreplaceable works of art.[xxxviii]

Years following the eruption, I received one of these pieces: a vibrant fuchsia heart webbed in color—turquois, ivory, sapphire and deep purple. Though beautiful, it never matched my neutral décor, so I placed it in a garage sale. After two sales, I finally received one offer:

"I don't need the heart—but I'll give you fifty cents for the brass hanger."

Are you kidding me?

Something in me rose up in defense of the unwanted heart. *"Oh—sorry. This is no longer for sale."*

I marched inside, giving it a prime location on my kitchen windowsill. One afternoon, sunlight ignited its fractured colors and I stood still, overwhelmed by its beauty.

Born from catastrophe—yet still radiant.

I recognized myself in that heart—my life was being forged through an unexpected blow. God, the Master Refiner, had not recreated my old life—He was creating a new one, revealing sacred details in small increments within my story. Over time, joy had trickled into my heart. Peace had found a home again. Hope replaced sighs of despair. Life had returned!

Thirty years after Mount St. Helen's eruption, one hiker said: "*I was in love with the way it was. I still am. But over time, that gave way to re-falling in love with the way it's coming back."*[xxxix]

I understood that.

After Karissa's death, life would never look the same—I grieved that deeply. But over time, I learned to trust God's ability to make it beautiful in a different way. He created beauty from the ashes. (See Isaiah 61:3)

Scientists later described Mount St. Helens with three words: Rebirth. Restoration. Recovery.

That is exactly what Jesus had done in my heart.

One journalist wrote, *"The reason this rebirth is so outstanding is because man has had nothing to do with it."*

Exactly. New life appeared because God brought it forth.

Your life will not look the same after loss. But as you entrust your ashes to His healing work, He will grow something new within you.

Keep returning to The Place. He restores. He brings beauty from devastation. And one day, you may whisper with quiet wonder, *Life has returned.*

Scripture urges us to fix our eyes on Jesus—the Author and Perfecter of our faith. He designed the blueprint of our lives before we lived one day. (See Psalm 139:16), and He promises to finish what He began. (See Philippians 1:6)

What would it mean to place the pen in His hands?

One of my most freeing prayers was this: *Merciful Creator, who am I to rewrite a story You already know? Today I surrender the editing of my life to You.*

Dashed dreams and broken hearts tempt us to cling to control—to hold the ashes of what was. The problem is, we can't forge anything beautiful from it. Our attempts remain limited—God-given purpose stays buried beneath the rubble.

But God—The Plac*e of Purpose*—forms strength from weakness, purpose from pain, and beauty from what we once believed beyond repair… and the life I thought had ended continues to bear fruit.

CHAPTER 29

WHEN THE ROCKS CRY OUT

"See, I am doing a new thing!
Now it springs up; do you not perceive it?
I am making a way in the wilderness
and streams in the wasteland."
Isaiah 43:19 (NIV)

Decades passed; God slowly restored what grief had shattered. He blessed us with children. Their lives have quietly echoed within these pages. Karissa's life didn't fade—it bore fruit. Our family witnessed God's tender care for broken hearts—His ability to produce fruit from famine seasons. Healing taught us to recognize God's presence not only in milestones—but in quiet, ordinary moments.

Gary and I enjoy hiking—nothing extreme… just an opportunity to step away from life's familiar noise to experience the stillness of God's creation. One fall morning, we tried a new trail in Eastern Washington. Crisp air and blazing leaves energized us. The trail led us to a cedar grove that appeared like something from a storybook—and long before we saw it, we heard it—the sound of water somewhere ahead pulled us onward.

When we reached it, the source surprised us. The stream was unimpressive. Yet as the water skipped across the rocks, it sang. Without those stones, the water would have flowed quietly past, unnoticed. Instead, every stone gave it voice.

I stood there listening—Amazed that something so unimpressive could resound like music simply because of what it struck along the way.

The image stayed with me. Those rocks…

Rocks often feel like the problem in a landscape—obstacles buried beneath the surface, breaking shovels and plans. In life they can signify the hidden nightmares within our stories: decisions that stubbed our soul, temptations that tripped us up, losses we never chose, grief that changed everything. We want them removed… or at least buried deep, where no one sees them.

But when the waters of God's mercy move across them, something changes.

Our wounds begin to witness.

The Psalmist asks, *"Has the Lord redeemed you? Then speak out!"* Psalm 107:1 (NLT)

He doesn't remove every stone. He redeems them. The painful places — once gray and heavy—begin to gleam within the current of His story. Each becomes a marker of where He met us… a stone to stand on when life trembles again. They speak out--a testimony of grace.

I still ask God to use the rocks of my own pain-filled journey, to allow them to keep singing—because others are walking behind me, limping across the sharp edges of their own stories.

I trust God to arrange them in a way that will produce a melody to soften their pain, pronouncing: *"He makes all things new."* (See Revelation 21:5).

Prone To Forget

Over the past three decades, God has patiently revealed more of Himself to me—not only through Scripture, but through lived experience. He has been *The Place* where I could carry every unwanted layer of pain. I sensed His longing for me to remain with Him. My suffering became an opportunity to understand, more than just ideas *about* Him, I was discovering Him—dimensions of His nature I had read about in Scripture, but now… I experienced.

He offered Himself: His Presence in the darkness. Peace when life made no sense. Provision to fill the emptiness. Perspective when everything felt foggy. Pardon when guilt squeezed. Protection when fear pressed in. Promises even when I doubted. Strength when my faith felt threadbare.

Time became a tutor, slowly confirming His trustworthy character. I had learned to stand on the bedrock of His love rather than on my emotions. Instead of listening to my soul, the Holy Spirit has counseled me to speak His Word over it—inviting His Truth to weave a counternarrative to my storyline.

Somewhere on that healing trail, God began to change me. Karissa's life—still as close as my next breath—carried purpose. Instead of staring at what tragedy had stolen, I found the God who never left when life erupted. Mere survival gave way to calling. The seasons—those chapters written in tears were not wasted. A new ache arose from deep within, a longing I hadn't known to walk alongside others carrying familiar pieces of a shattered heart.

So, on that path, I began to collect stones. Literal rocks. I call them memorial stones—markers of a journey marked by God's hand. On each stone I record a circumstance that rocked us and the way God intervened. My rocks sit in a bowl, a quiet testimony:

Life crushed—but God repaired.

Life unraveled—but God wrote a better story.

Deep waters threatened—but God reached in.

They offer an opportunity to share God's faithfulness in hard times. Telling those stories becomes fresh bread—meant to be enjoyed and shared with others.

Mark Batterson writes, *"Everyone wants a miracle. But here's the catch: no one wants to be in a situation that necessitates one! Of course, you can't have one without the other. The prerequisite for a miracle is a problem..."*[xl]

And—life never runs out of problems. I'm still learning to invite God into them—and then to wait and watch for Him.

I borrowed the idea of collecting stones from Joshua. He received God's pep talk in chapter twenty-seven: *Be strong and courageous—I'll never leave or forsake you.* God made that promise while Joshua and over a million Israelites stood on the wrong side of a flooded river that separated them from the promised land. They couldn't cross it without catastrophic loss.

Enter God. The river split, and where water had rushed moments earlier, a new generation felt dry ground under their feet. After crossing, Joshua gathered twelve men to go back into the middle of that riverbed. Each man was instructed to grab a large stone to build a memorial to God. I wonder if they looked at all the stones on the hillside and questioned why they couldn't use one of them.

I imagine Joshua guided those thoughts: *We'll select a rock from the place God revealed His strength and involvement in the deepest waters of our story.* These rocks were carried to the banks of their new home—the first architectural structure in the Promised Land was a memorial to remember what God had done. It would keep this iconic day from fading.

I feel the same way. I am prone to forget God's manifold miracles. My mind is like a colander—holding on to what I need to release and losing what I long to remember. These simple stones help me recall God's involvement in stories I can't afford to forget.

I've always loved Moses' final instructions before he died:

"Only be careful, and watch yourselves closely so that you
do not forget the things your eyes have seen
or let them fade from your heart as long as you live.
Teach them to your children
and to their children after them.
Deuteronomy 4:9 (NIV)

What we use matters less than *that* we remember—a journal, a photo of something symbolic—anything that ties our story to God's faithfulness within it.

Remembering strengthens our faith when fear rises. God never runs out of ways to remind us: He's in the mess with us.

God has redeemed my broken story—not by erasing it, but by restoring it.

He has used a repaired life—not a perfect one, to testify of His glory.

And the retelling of His faithfulness becomes an inheritance for those who come after me. Because when the rocks cry out, future generations turn to listen.

CHAPTER 30

A DOORWAY OF HOPE

O my Strength, I will sing praises to you,
for you, O God, are my fortress,
the God who shows me steadfast love.
Psalm 59:17 (ESV)

A Doorway Of Hope

Five years before losing Karissa, I was a single, nineteen-year-old, sitting beside my boyfriend, Gary, near the back of our college chapel. I was wearing my favorite corduroy red jumper and an expectant smile. Wednesdays were a welcome pause in our academic routine—ninety minutes set aside to gather with classmates for a refreshing time of worship and inspiration from the Word. Usually, a professor spoke. Occasionally, a guest speaker visited. Today was one of those special occasions.

Evangelist Dick Mills had a reputation for opening Scripture in ways that stirred both conviction and healing. I had grown up believing God spoke personally through His Word, but I had never been in a setting where the Word was used prophetically to give affirmation and direction to specific individuals.

As the Word fell like rain over our weary souls, it stirred a hunger for more of God. After teaching, the speaker began praying for individuals. We weren't sure what to expect:

"*Young lady in the back.*"

He was looking in my direction. I turned around. No one stood behind me.

"Yes—you in the red jumper. Please stand."

Why was I already crying?

"*You love God deeply. He has drawn you to Himself since you were a child."*

It was true. My heart pounded. Tears blurred the room. God had my full attention.

"In the days ahead, your love for Him will be severely tested. But do not fear—He will be with you. Your love will be refined in the fire, and afterward it will shine like pure gold. One day women will come to you, asking 'Please show me Jesus like you know Him.' Your hands will touch His children, becoming instruments of healing."

I was silenced. Chapel ended. I skipped lunch and ran straight to the prayer tower with my journal. I wrote every word I could remember. After writing them down, I closed my eyes. The tears fell. "Jesus…" I didn't know what else to say.

Finally, I re-read the words… over and over.

At nineteen, the words that pierced my heart had nothing to do with future ministry. I was gripped by, *'You will be severely tested...'*

"God, I don't know how to prepare for—that. What if I'm not ready?"

I don't think any of us are truly ready for the trials we try to imagine. God doesn't give imaginary grace for imagined pain. He gives real grace when real pain arrives.

Life moved forward. Gary proposed. We married and graduated the next year. Then, we stepped into ministry. Soon after, I became pregnant and delivered a healthy baby girl—Karissa.

The prophecy had long faded into the background. I assumed the "severe testing" referred to the tumors discovered on my pituitary during my junior year. Though it was hard to leave school, to explore our medical options, the trial hadn't been as severe as I thought it would. I was grateful. Maybe later I would witness the way God brought something valuable from it.

Years later, broken in the aftermath of Karissa's death—the words returned with piercing clarity:

You will be severely tested. Oh God. I was living it.

I anchored to what I remembered of His promise when everything felt like it was dissolving. God had foreseen this fire. He had promised to stay with me in it. This thought was the only thing that steadied me when the ground beneath me crumbled.

I clung—sometimes fiercely, sometimes barely—to the promise that this suffering would not destroy my love for Him but deepen it.

Job voiced that same conviction:

But he knows the way that I take;
when he has tested me, I will come forth as gold.
Job 23:10 (NIV)

...He controls my destiny.
Job 23:14b (NLT)

He did not let the furnace of affliction destroy me. I wasn't scorched by its flames. I do not even carry the lingering smell of smoke.

My love for Him *did* grow stronger—not because I was strong—but because He never let go.

He stayed in the darkness.

He received my questions.

He gathered every fragment of faith I dropped along the way.

He rescued me when I fell, and carried me when there were no steps left within me.

He became for me, *My Place of Refuge, and* invited me to stay forever.

His refining was not swift. I often wondered if it would ever end, I'm not sure it ever will. But slowly—beyond the ashes, I recognized beauty surrounding me. Joy surprised me. Hope returned. My life was anchored deeply in His love.

Then something unexpected began to happen. Purpose began to unfold. Calls started coming. *"Would you come and share how you made it through your suffering?"* Ironically, I wasn't sure I had '*made it through'*, but I was honored to talk about the intimacy of God's presence while walking it out. I did not desire a platform. I didn't feel qualified to share. I still don't. When I respond to an invitation, it is with the very real conviction that Jesus wants to heal hearts… and He is giving me the honor of joining Him in what He is about to do.

He alone holds the words of eternal life. In the same way He fed thousands with five loaves and two fish, He receives the stories we offer Him. When placed in His hands, they are transformed, becoming miraculous bread to share. And in the sharing, others taste and see how good God is.

During these past years, David's words burned deep in my soul:

For you have been my hope, Sovereign Lord,
my confidence since my youth.

I have become a sign to many;
you are my strong refuge.
My mouth will tell of your righteous deeds,
of your saving acts all day long—
though I know not how to relate them all.
Since my youth, God, you have taught me,
and to this day I declare your marvelous deeds.
Even when I am old and gray,
do not forsake me, my God,
till I declare your power to the next generation,
your mighty acts to all who are to come.
Psalm 71:5,7, 15, 17-18 (NIV)

I read these words with awe. Our limitations do not surprise God. He is glorified through them. He empowers us—mere humans—to declare His faithful, truthful, powerful, lovely, intimate and constant presence in the darkest parts of our story. God is beyond description. My heart resonates deeply with David's words: *"I don't know how to relate it all."* But, I will keep trying as long as I live.

I recognize His healing power wasn't solely for my benefit—though He cares greatly about me. It was more than that.

Jesus invites those of us who have experienced His grace, to become ambassadors of grace, to comfort and care for His broken and bleeding lambs, and to bind up all their wounds. What a privilege He has invited me into—to help others discover His presence when storms rage and to know His voice when the flood waters threaten.

I no longer wish to remove pages from my story. Those pages are sacred places where Jesus searched for me—the ways His unhindered love broke through barriers to find me where I lay. He carried me when I was too weak to stand and held me close so I could know His heart—the heart of the Shepherd.

He promises:

I will lead her into the wilderness
and speak tenderly to her.
There I will give her back her vineyards
and will make the Valley of Achor a door of hope.
Hosea 2:14b-15a (NIV)

The Valley of Achor means The Valley of Trouble. It was marked with disobedience, defeat, despair, and death. But into a valley that held nothing but painful memories, God promised something new—He would change it into a gateway of hope.

He doesn't erase our valley or deny the pain we experienced there, but He rebuilds our future starting right where everything fell apart.

Our stories become a gateway of hope, not only for ourselves but for others stuck in their pain, loss and shame. I prayerfully await the day when you sense your own pain transforming into something new. *The Place of Purpose* turns barren valleys into fertile ground and causes joy to overflow from shattered stories.

My story has not demonstrated a short-cut through suffering. I never outgrew my need for God—I never will. He alone is My Place—the Refuge I choose to remain in. I need Him now as much as I needed Him then. I realize how barren and brittle my life is when I attempt to walk life's journey alone.

Your journey may be strikingly different from mine. Our common factor is *the Familiar Friend* who will venture down the trail beside you, every step of the way.

Vulneratus Non Victus

Betrayal, loss, disease, death—they may wound us, but they do not get the final word over a life hidden in Christ.

As this book comes to a close, I will leave you with my family motto. Beneath my family's *O'Grady* crest—my maiden name—are the Latin words:

Vulneratus non Victus: Wounded, Not Conquered.

The battles we walk through leave scars. I often wonder if those scars are the one thing we will carry into heaven. Jesus did. His resurrected body still bore the marks in His hands and feet and the wound in His side. He invited His followers to touch them.

Scars tell a story—not only of what hurt us, but what God redeemed. Mine will always remind me of our little girl whose life forever shaped mine, the sorrow of losing her, and a faithful God who met me in the aftermath and ascribed value to my shattered heart.

I was wounded in suffering—but not conquered. *I am more than a conqueror through Christ who loves me."* (personalized - Romans 8:37)

God forms our stories into something meant to be shared—like a book to be read; like music carried on stones placed within the current of His grace. My prayer is that these pages have offered hope to comfort your despair, salve to soothe your wounds, and a doorway inviting you into something invitingly new in Christ.

As you look back over these encounters, may you recognize the God who smashes gates of bronze and cuts through bars of iron to reach you where you are. He offers you rare treasures only found in dark places. (See Isaiah 45:2-3)

One day, you may begin to discover purpose woven through your suffering—though today that may feel impossible to imagine. The good news is you don't have to create that purpose. Jesus already holds it.

For now, hoist your sails to the wind of His Spirit and let Him become your refuge, *your Place of Safety*. (Psalm 91:1)

Beauty awaits,

Patty

INVITING GOD TO BECOME YOUR PLACE OF PURPOSE

As you come to the end of this book, I pray this final journaling section would lead you to the realization that your story still has a future—prepared by God.

You may still be guarding wounds that cause you to wince when touched. The intent of this book isn't to push you toward a swift healing. Jesus cares more about the authentic healing of your heart. Perhaps you are hoping time will dull the sting that continues to exacerbate your pain. Or maybe you desire to place your festering wounds and broken heart in Jesus' hands, allowing them to become part of the story He is redeeming.

Regardless of where you find yourself, I pray you recognize you are profoundly loved by a Shepherd who will always search for you where you have fallen and will stay with you right where life crumbled around you.

Take a deep breath. Then slowly exhale. You belong here... in The Place. He loves you right where you are right now.

Naming your Wound—Without Fear

If your scars could speak, what would they say about the story you have lived through?

I often discovered God was nearer than I realized at the time. What might your scars also say about God's faithfulness toward you?

In describing his suffering, Paul wrote: *"We are hard pressed on every side, but not crushed... struck down, but not destroyed."* 2 Corinthians 4:8–9 (NIV)

As you read that passage, is there a prayer that may be rising up within you?

Remembering the Valley

What once felt like my ending, slowly became a doorway of something new—Hope. Are there any moments on your journey where you have felt God stepped into your Valley of Trouble, offering a doorway to something new?

Listening for the Song

God doesn't discard the chapters written in sorrow. He slowly gathers them—stones in a riverbed—and then commands His mercy and love to rush over them, producing a song from our sorrow. Has any part of your pain shaped a new song of praise, compassion, tenderness, wisdom, or strength?

A Prayer through all the Pain

Oh Father,
You have never shifted away from the wounds I still guard.
Thank You for not turning away from my sorrow.
Instead, You chose to stay—becoming My Place…
Presence in the pressing darkness.
Peace to my anxious heart.
Provision for my deep longing.
Protection surrounding me in all my fear.
Pardon when guilt threatened to separate me from You.
Perspective when I lost my way.
Promise to steady by faltering faith.

Power to equip me in my weakness.
Purpose through all my pain.

You never stop redeeming those areas I allow You to touch,
You transform my troubles into a doorway —of hope and into a deeper life with You.
Teach me to trust that my scars hold valueg serving as reminders that Your nearness made me new.
I was wounded… but never conquered.
Not because I am strong, but because You are that good!
And so…I trust when I cannot see…
Beauty Still Awaits,

Forever Yours, _______________

ACKNOWLEDGEMENTS

How can I begin to express the overflowing gratitude to everyone who helped breathe this book into existence? The impression to write this book was whispered into my soul a few years after Karissa's death. God kept the dream alive on this long journey. Writing it has been an act of obedience to a call I never let go of.

These were not wasted years. They were discoveries of Living Water in the most obscure places. God drew near in the darkness. He proved His steadfast love in more ways than I can possibly trace.

This story is my attempt to shine a light on the beauty of His presence. He never stopped breathing on the embers—never allowed the fire to dim. His faithful presence kept the vision of this book before me so that others might know how trustworthy He is, even in life's hardest moments.

Jesus often revealed Himself most through the people who joined me on my journey through the years. I am convinced this book would still be tangled in dozens of journals had it not been for those who gently nudged me to retrace and compile the story.

Foremost, I thank my beloved Gary. You have been the quiet strength on every page of our story. Your hands are the ones God used to tenderly hold my broken heart. Your steadfast belief in God's calling on my life has been one of His greatest gifts to me.

Your encouragement went far beyond words. You saw me as an author long before I became one, even surprising me with a writing desk. You arranged writing retreats and even a trip to Washington, D.C. so I could learn from one of my favorite authors, Mark

Batterson. Who knew how instrumental that meeting would be in helping me find my way through the writing forest. Somehow, deep in your bones, you believed that this book would one day be written... even when I began to wonder if God might change His mind and invite me to do something easier.

Thank you for never giving up on me… or on us.

And to *our Fabulous Four*—Hannah, Kassie, Kolton, and Briley—you are living proof that Jesus knows the deepest longing of our hearts. Being chosen as your mom has always been my highest calling and the greatest honor Jesus could entrust to me.

Thank you for so willingly giving me space to enter the quiet place to know Him more. I needed His life alive in me to offer even a marred reflection of His love for you. He has not only revealed Himself to me—we will never run out of reasons to celebrate the manifold ways He made Himself real to every one of us. Oh, the stories we could tell… perhaps we'll save those for another book.

To our beloved Tujunga church family—thank you for being there in the first raw moments of our tragedy. You chose to be crammed into that small waiting room and stood beside us—waiting with us—holding our bleeding hearts when our world fell apart.

To my family – you flew across the nation to hold our broken hearts. I love you.

To Dan Lelacheur—you were our first call when Karissa was pronounced dead. We needed to talk to someone who had lived through catastrophic loss. Thank you for taking that call. You were right. We did find beauty beyond the wilderness. Jesus really does heal broken hearts.

To My dear Tujunga Sisters of the Heart—Wanda, Julie, Cindee, Dorothy, Brendi, Laura, Julie, Robin—you put your families on hold to hold me. You stayed when it would have been much easier to run the other way. Thank you for offering your presence, day after day, becoming healing balm for my gaping wound.

To Heidi Brown—thank you for responding to the Holy Spirit by sending Scriptures in the mail with my name written into them. Those precious, cut-outs—hearts, lambs and bears—literally carried the words of eternal life into the deep places of my broken heart. They kept me alive when hope failed. God etched these promises across my heart. They show up in various messages I shared around the world. Many of them made their way into this book.

To Zola Thompson—thank you. Your obedience revealed a counter-narrative woven within my suffering. Your willingness to respond to God's voice allowed me to know, without doubt, that He truly sees. He listens. He cares. And He stoops into our shattered circumstances, reclaiming our past and rewriting our futures. Only heaven knows the countless number of people whose hearts have been made new by Jesus intimate love, made evident through one servant, willing to deliver a message of life to a broken, young mommy that Mother's Day so many years ago.

To all the Pastors and Leaders—you believed that God could speak through this ordinary vessel—thank you. God's faithfulness never fails.

To Mark Batterson—your words, published in so many books, are stamped on my heart and echoed within these pages. Your encouraging words during this writing journey has given me courage when I needed it. You have been a miracle on this journey—a mile-marker of God's presence cheering me on in this God-sized assignment. JEJIT—always.

To Clara Rose and the Rosedale Publishing Team—thank you for believing in this book as much as I did. Thank you for your patience with my endless questions (now you know how to pray for my family). Your timely ideas helped shape this book into something I never dreamed possible. Your calm assurance throughout this journey has been a gift.

To the Anonymous Donor who miraculously provided what was needed for this book to be completed—you partnered with the Holy Spirit like a watchman on a wall. Seeing further than most could imagine, you caught a glimpse of what God might do through this book and generously celebrated His work in and through me. Though I may never know who you are, Jesus does—and He applauds you. Thank you for helping place this book into the hands of people carrying busted hearts and broken stories.

To my Beta Reading Group—you were the faithful midwives surrounding me through the final stages of labor. You helped me keep the long vision in mind until this book was finally born. Anyone who reads this book receives something refined by your collective wisdom and honest feedback. Thank you: Jodi Detrick, Sue Reeve, Stephanie Lovell, Gail Johnsen, Denise Robinson, Mandy Offield, Kelly Murray, Dakotah Murphy, Hannah Garvey and Kassie Moreno—You made the impossible possible.

And finally, to Kolton and Briley Moreno—That cover! **Kolton and Dallas**, thank you for putting your genius creativity to work to design the cover. It is incredible. **And Briley,** Thank you for pouring your heart over this book through a canvas, oil paints, and brush strokes. Your prayerfully painted lamb captures the heart of this book, and I believe the heart of many stories. Whether readers see themselves through the lamb— lying helpless with their own shattered stories, or they see the perfect Lamb of God who was broken and slain for our redemption… your painting speaks beyond words.

Jesus, receive all the glory,

Patty

ABOUT THE AUTHOR

Patty Moreno is a speaker, author, and pastor of spiritual formation. She shares messages of hope and healing with audiences around the world, carrying a special passion for those who know the deep ache of suffering.

Patty and her husband, Gary, live in Liberty Lake, Washington. Together they planted Legacy Church, where they have the joy of testifying to a God who reclaims our past and rewrites our future.

Their greatest joy is spending time with their four married children and seven grandchildren.

A Personal Note

If this book found its way into your hands, chances are you have walked through places you never planned to go.

I wrote *The Place* because I needed a companion when my own world shattered. I longed to hear from someone who had walked through suffering and discovered that God had not abandoned them there.

If the pages of this book stirred something tender in your story, I want you to know: you are not alone. I would love to continue walking with you.

To learn more or to schedule Patty to speak at one of your events go to: www.pattymoreno.org

Email at: pattymorenobooks@gmail.com

www.PattyMoreno.org

Listen to messages at:
https://www.youtube.com/@LegacyChurchWa

ENDNOTES

---

[i] Chapter 1: ***The Twilight Zone*** is an American Science fiction television series created by Rod Serling. Five seasons ran from 1959-1964. https://en.wikipedia.org/wiki/The_Twilight_Zone

[ii] Chapter 2: A rare condition known as hematohidrosis. US National Library of Medicine, Journal List, Indian J Dermatol, v 54(3); Jul-Sep 2009. PMC2810702 (https://www.ncbi.nlm.nih.gov/pmc/articles/PMC2810702/)

[iii] Chapter 2: Wiersbe, W. W. (1996). *The Bible exposition commentary* (Vol. 1, p. 268). Wheaton, IL: Victor Books.

[iv] Chapter 2: Jesus calls himself the gate in John 10 (CSB)

[v] Chapter 3: Moreno, Gary. Lord Receive Her. 1986

[vi] Chapter 3: Description of death in 1 Corinthians 15:9-10

[vii] Chapter 3: A Journal for the Expectant Mother. ©Patty Moreno. Oct 22, 1985.

[viii] Chapter 4: https://healthypsych.com/navigating-the-dark-night-of-the-soul/ Chiara Viscomi, Feb 26, 2016.

[ix] Keller, Phillip. *A Shepherd's Look at Psalm 23.* Grand Rapids, Zondervan Publishing House, 1970.

[x] Chapter 4: https://healthypsych.com/navigating-the-dark-night-of-the-soul/F. Scott Fitzgerald, *The Crack-Up*

[xi] Chapter 4: Phillip Keller. *A Shepherd's Look at Psalm 23.* Grand Rapids, Zondervan Publishing House, 1970.

[xii] Chapter 4: Erwin McManus. *"The Power of Resilience"*. Series: The Path to Inner Peace, Mosaic, Hollywood, CA, May 10, 2020

[xiii] Chapter 5: V. Raymond Edman, Wheaton College President, Illinois 1941-1965

[xiv] Chapter 7: Ann Voskamp, *The Greatest Gift: Unwrapping the Full Love Story of Christmas* (Nashville: Tyndale House Publishers, 2014), 79.

[xv] Chapter 7: Jerry Sittser, *A Grace Disguised* (Grand Rapids, Michigan: Zondervan, 1995, 2004) Jerry Sittser, *A Grace Disguised* (Grand Rapids, Michigan: Zondervan, 1995, 2004). 22.

[xvi] Chapter 7: Spurgeon cited in https://www.blueletterbible.org/Comm/guzik_david/StudyGuide2017-Jam/Jam-1.cfm?a=1147003

[xvii] Chapter 10: Johnson, Nicole. *Fresh Brewed Life: a stirring invitation to wake up your soul.* (Nashville, Thomas Nelson, 1999, 2011)

[xviii] Chapter 10: Bill Johnson, https://prayer-coach.com/2012/03/26/bill-johnson-quotes/

[xix] Chapter 10: Cornwall, Judson. *Praying The Scriptures: Using God's Words to Effect Change in All of Life's Situations.* Lake Mary, Charisma House Book Club, 1988.

[xx] Chapter 11: Crowe, Kelsey and Emily McDowell. *There is No Good Card for This.* (San Francisco, Harper One), 2017.

[xxi] Chapter 11: Kittel, Gerhard, et al. *Theological Dictionary of the Old Testament.* Freedman, David Noel, ed. *The Anchor Bible Dictionary.* Cross, Frank Moore. *Canaanite Myth and Hebrew Epic.*

[xxii] Chapter 11: Lockyer, Herbert. *All the Divine Names and Titles in the Bible.* (Grand Rapids, Zondervan, 1975). 14.

[xxiii] Chapter 12: Mark Batterson, Wild Goose Chase: Reclaim the Adventure of Pursuing God (Colorado Springs, CO: Multnomah Books, 2008), 79.

[xxiv] Chapter 13: https://believersportal.com/list-365-fear-not-bible-verses/

[xxv] Chapter 16: Henri J.M. Nouwen, *Life of the Beloved: Spiritual Living in a Secular World,* (New York: The Crossroad Publishing Company, 1992), 33.

[xxvi] Chapter 17: [xxvi] https://www.ministrymagazine.org/archive/1950/09/the-story-of-the-love-of-god

[xxvii] Chapter 18: Lysa TerKeurst, *It's Not supposed to Be This Way,* (Nashville: Nelson Books, 2018) 145.

[xxviii] Chapter 19: https://www.insightvisioncenter.com/human-vision-vs-eagle-vision/July 8, 2016

[xxix] Chapter 19: Batterson, Mark, *In A Pit With A Lion On A Snowy Day* (Colorado Springs: Multnomah Books, 2006) 64.

[xxx] Chapter 20: Lusko, Levi, *Through the Eyes of a Lion,* Nashville: Thomas Nelson, 2015) 37

[xxxi] Chapter 20: Moreno, Patty. Journal entry, May 8, 1987

[xxxii] Chapter 21: John Stott, The Cross of Christ (Downers Grove, IL: InterVarsity Press, 1986) p335-336.

[xxxiii] Chapter 23: Knowles, Victor (1998) *"Promise and Fulfillment: Believing the Promises of God," Leaven: Vol. 6: Iss. 3, Article 4. Available at: https://digitalcommons.pepperdine.edu/leaven/vol6/iss3/4*

[xxxiv] Chapter 26: To learn more about how to hear God's voice I recommend *Whisper*, by Mark Batterson and *How to Hear God* by Pete Greig.

[xxxv] Chapter 26: Eric Metaxas, *Bonhoeffer* (Nashville: Thomas Nelson, 2010, 2020) p 128.

[xxxvi] Chapter 28: Katherine and Jay Wolf, Hope Heals; Suffer Strong (Grand Rapids: Zondervan, 2016, 2020).

[xxxvii] Chapter 28: Brennan Manning, The Signature of Jesus (Colorado Springs: Multnoma, 1996) 98-99.

[xxxviii] Chapter 28: https://www.pacificnorthwestshop.com/shop-by-theme/glass-eye-studio-mt-st-helens-volcanic-ash-hand-blown-glass.html

[xxxix] Chapter 28: [xxxix] The Coeur d'Alene Press, May 18, 2010, newspaper clipping commemorating the explosion's 30th anniversary.

[xl] Chapter 29: Mark Batterson, *The Grave Robber: How Jesus Can Make Your Impossible Possible* (Grand Rapids, MI: Baker Books, 2014) 16.

www.ingramcontent.com/pod-product-compliance
Lightning Source LLC
LaVergne TN
LVHW100516110826
845146LV00002B/668

* 9 7 9 8 9 9 9 8 7 9 6 3 9 *